THRIVING AT WORK

The Power of Physical Well-Being

Gitangshu Adhikary

Preface

Never before has the well-being of employees been more critical. As the boundaries between our professional and personal lives continue to blur, the need for a holistic approach to health has emerged as a cornerstone of successful organizations. Thriving at Work: The Power of Physical Well-Being is an exploration of this essential connection between physical health and overall productivity, job satisfaction, and emotional resilience.

The journey to well-being begins with an understanding of the foundational principles that govern our physical health. In the opening chapters, we delve into the profound impact that maintaining physical well-being can have on our emotional and mental states. Supported by compelling statistics and real-life examples from renowned organizations, we see how a strong commitment to physical health not only enhances individual performance but also fosters a vibrant workplace culture.

Throughout this book, I emphasize the mind-body connection —a relationship that is pivotal for both mental and physical health. The power of exercise, nutrition, hydration, and sleep are examined in detail, illustrating how these elements intertwine to create a framework for success. I share testimonies from employees who have transformed their work experience through simple lifestyle adjustments, proving that small changes can yield significant results.

Recognizing the diverse challenges employees face in prioritizing their health, I provide practical strategies for integrating wellness into daily routines. From time management techniques to finding enjoyable forms of exercise, this book offers actionable insights designed to help you thrive amidst the demands of work and life.

Moreover, Thriving at Work extends beyond individual wellness; it highlights the critical role organizations play in fostering a culture of health. Leaders are encouraged to champion wellness initiatives that engage and inspire employees, leading to higher retention rates and improved morale. The inclusion of case studies and real-world examples brings these concepts to life, showcasing the transformative potential of workplace wellness programs.

As we navigate the complexities of modern work life, let this book serve as a guide and an inspiration. Whether you are an employee seeking to enhance your well-being or a leader striving to create a supportive work environment, the principles outlined within these pages will empower you to take actionable steps toward a healthier, more fulfilling work life.

Together, let us embark on this journey toward thriving at work —where physical well-being is not just a goal, but a way of life.

WHO THIS BOOK IS FOR

Thriving at Work: The Power of Physical Well-Being is for anyone who understands that a healthy body is the foundation for a successful and fulfilling career. Whether you're a business leader looking to boost team productivity, an HR professional designing employee wellness programs, or an individual seeking to improve your own physical well-being amidst a busy work schedule, this book provides the insights and strategies you need.

Managers and Business Leaders who want to create a culture of health and wellness that enhances both team performance and employee satisfaction.

HR Professionals and workplace wellness advocates seeking practical, evidence-based tools to promote physical health, reduce stress, and foster long-term productivity.

Employees at any level who are juggling professional demands and personal well-being, and are looking for actionable tips to stay fit, energized, and mentally sharp while succeeding at work.

Anyone interested in the powerful connection between physical health and professional success, and in learning how small lifestyle changes can lead to big improvements in performance and job satisfaction.

ABOUT THE AUTHOR

Gitangshu Adhikary is a passionate advocate for workplace wellness and employee well-being. With years of experience consulting for organizations on employee health initiatives and workplace culture, he has seen firsthand the transformative power of integrating physical well-being into professional environments. His expertise spans across corporate wellness programs, productivity enhancement, and fostering sustainable work-life balance.

In Thriving at Work: The Power of Physical Well-Being, Gitangshu combines his deep understanding of organizational behavior with the latest research on health and performance. He provides actionable strategies to help companies create thriving, healthier workforces, and empowers individuals to boost their physical health and professional success.

A sought-after speaker and wellness strategist, Gitangshu is dedicated to inspiring leaders and employees alike to prioritize their physical well-being as a pathway to sustained performance and fulfillment at work.

DEDICATION

To my teachers and professors, for instilling in me the value of balance and well-being in every aspect of life.

To my mentors, whose guidance and support have shaped my understanding of what it means to truly thrive.

And to all the leaders, teams, and individuals committed to fostering healthier, happier workplaces—this book is for you. May it inspire and empower you to prioritize physical well-being, not just for success at work, but for a more fulfilling life.

ACKNOWLE DGEMENT

Writing Thriving at Work: The Power of Physical Well-Being has been a journey made possible by the support and encouragement of many people, to whom I am deeply grateful.

First and foremost, I would like to thank my family for their unwavering belief in me. Krishna and Chandramouli, your love, patience, and encouragement have been my anchor throughout this process.

To my colleagues, mentors, and clients who have shared their insights and experiences on workplace wellness—I am indebted to you for shaping my understanding of the powerful connection between health and performance. Your stories of success and challenge have been invaluable.

A special thanks to the companies and organizations who opened their doors and shared their wellness journeys with me. Your willingness to experiment with new ideas and prioritize employee health serves as an inspiration and a model for others to follow.

I am also grateful to the researchers and experts whose work has laid the foundation for this book. Your dedication to exploring the science of well-being and productivity has made this book richer and more grounded in evidence.

Finally, to my readers—thank you for picking up this book and embarking on the journey to create healthier, more vibrant workplaces. May the strategies and stories in these pages inspire you to thrive, both at work and in life.

CHAPTER 1: THE FOUNDATIO N OF WELL- BEING

When it comes to well-being, the foundation is built upon one crucial element: physical health. Imagine your body as a finely tuned machine. Every cog, every bolt, and every wire plays a vital role in ensuring smooth operation. If one part falters, the entire system can suffer. Similarly, your physical health is the bedrock that supports your emotional and mental well-being. Without it, stress can become overwhelming, focus can wane, and productivity can plummet.

Physical health isn't merely about the absence of illness; it encompasses a vibrant state of wellness that fosters resilience against life's inevitable challenges. When you prioritize your physical health, you're not just investing in your body; you're also investing in your mind and emotions. Research shows that a healthy body translates to a healthier mind, reducing anxiety and depression and enhancing your overall mood. It allows you to approach challenges with a clearer perspective, enabling you to respond rather than react.

Now, let's take a closer look at the connection between physical health and job performance. Statistics tell a powerful story. A study published in the Harvard Business Review revealed a striking correlation between high physical health ratings and job productivity. Employees who maintained good physical health reported productivity levels that were 30% higher than their less healthy counterparts. This staggering figure is not just a number; it signifies the tremendous impact that prioritizing physical well-being can have on your professional life. Imagine what a 30% boost in productivity could mean for your career! More successful projects, increased recognition from peers and superiors, and the satisfaction of achieving your goals with greater ease.

Moreover, when employees invest in their physical health, the benefits extend far beyond individual productivity. Organizations see reduced absenteeism, lower healthcare costs, and enhanced employee morale. Companies that champion health and wellness initiatives foster environments where employees thrive, leading to higher retention rates and a positive workplace culture. This cycle of health and performance creates a win-win scenario for both employees and employers.

So, how can you harness the power of physical well-being to elevate your professional life? Start by making conscious choices that prioritize your health. This doesn't mean you have to overhaul your lifestyle overnight. Instead, think of it as a journey, taking small steps toward a healthier you. Perhaps you can commit to a short daily workout, replace one unhealthy snack with a nutritious option, or ensure you get enough sleep each night. Each of these choices adds up, creating a solid foundation for your overall well-being.

The path to improved physical health doesn't have to be daunting. With each positive choice you make, you're investing in your potential. Picture yourself feeling energized, focused, and capable of handling any challenge that comes your way. That's the power of physical health—when you prioritize your well-being, you're not just surviving; you're thriving.

As you embark on this journey, remember: your body is your greatest asset. Treat it with care, respect, and love. Invest in it. Embrace the transformative effects of prioritizing your physical health, and watch as it spills over into every aspect of your life —emotional resilience, mental clarity, and, most importantly, your professional success.

Now is the time to take charge of your health. Stand up, stretch, take a deep breath, and let's move forward together. The foundation of well-being is within your grasp, and a vibrant, fulfilling life awaits you!

CHAPTER 2: THE MIND-BODY CONNECTION

Have you ever felt a surge of happiness after a good workout? That exhilarating feeling isn't just your imagination; it's the mind-body connection in action. Physical activity has an incredible influence on our mental health, acting as a natural antidote to stress, anxiety, and depression. When we engage in regular exercise, we aren't just strengthening our bodies; we're also nurturing our minds, creating a powerful synergy that enhances our overall well-being.

Let's start by understanding how physical activity boosts our mood. When you exercise, your body releases a cocktail of feel-good chemicals known as endorphins. Often referred to as "the body's natural painkillers," these endorphins interact with the receptors in your brain, reducing the perception of pain and triggering a positive feeling in the body. This is the "runner's high" that many athletes talk about—a euphoric state that can last for hours after a workout. But the benefits don't stop there; regular physical activity also stimulates the production of serotonin and dopamine, neurotransmitters that play a crucial role in regulating mood, emotions, and feelings of happiness.

Neuroscience has unveiled fascinating insights into the brain chemistry changes that occur with regular exercise. When you engage in physical activity, your brain undergoes profound transformations. Research shows that exercise increases the volume of the hippocampus, the part of the brain responsible for memory and learning. This growth is crucial, as it allows us to process information more effectively and reduces the risk of cognitive decline as we age. Additionally, exercise enhances neuroplasticity—the brain's ability to form new connections—making it easier for us to adapt to new challenges. In simpler terms, the more we move, the sharper our minds become.

But let's ground these scientific concepts with real-life experiences. Take Sarah, a marketing executive who found herself struggling with stress and anxiety due to the demands of her job. After a particularly overwhelming week, she decided to lace up her running shoes and hit the pavement. What started as a simple way to clear her mind transformed into a vital part of her routine. "Running has become my therapy," Sarah says. "After just a few minutes, I feel my worries start to fade. It's as if I'm shedding the weight of the day with each step." Over time, Sarah not only noticed her mood improving, but her job satisfaction skyrocketed. She became more focused, more creative, and more engaged in her work.

Then there's David, who turned to yoga after realizing that his high-stress job was taking a toll on his mental health. Initially hesitant, David joined a local class, and the results were life-changing. "Yoga taught me to breathe through my stress," he shares. "I learned to connect my body and mind, which made handling tough situations at work so much easier. Now, I approach challenges with a sense of calm rather than panic." Like Sarah, David found that the regular practice of physical activity didn't just improve his mood; it also enriched his overall job experience, allowing him to excel in his career.

These stories illustrate a profound truth: when we prioritize physical activity, we're not just enhancing our physical well-being; we're creating a solid foundation for mental resilience and job satisfaction. The mind-body connection is a powerful tool that can propel us toward success in both our personal and professional lives.

So, how can you harness this connection? Start by incorporating regular exercise into your routine—find an activity you enjoy, whether it's running, dancing, swimming, or practicing yoga. Even short bursts of movement can make a difference; aim for at least 30 minutes a day, and watch as your mood begins to shift, anxiety diminishes, and your job performance improves.

As you embark on this journey, remember that your mind and body are allies in your quest for a fulfilling life. Embrace the power of movement and allow it to elevate your spirit, sharpen your mind, and enhance your performance. The road to improved mental health is not only attainable; it's waiting for you to take the first step. Get moving, and let the incredible benefits of the mind-body connection lead you toward a more vibrant and rewarding life!

CHAPTER 3: WHY YOUR BODY MATTERS

In the world of business, every company aspires to achieve peak productivity, but what many don't realize is that the foundation for success lies not just in strategy or technology but in the health of its most valuable asset: its employees. When we talk about performance, we can no longer overlook the impact of physical health. The correlation between a healthy workforce and high productivity is not just a theory; it's a reality that can shape the future of any organization.

Let's take a moment to reflect on the undeniable truth: poor physical health can lead to a cascade of negative consequences for both employees and employers. Consider this:

when employees feel unwell—whether due to chronic illnesses, fatigue, or stress—they are less likely to be engaged in their work. This disengagement manifests as decreased productivity, increased absenteeism, and ultimately higher healthcare costs. The financial implications are staggering; organizations may find themselves grappling with the ripple effects of a workforce that is not functioning at its best.

A study published in the Harvard Business Review revealed some eye-opening statistics: employees with poor health are two to three times more likely to take sick days than their healthier counterparts. Furthermore, the financial burden on companies due to healthcare expenses related to chronic diseases can soar into the millions. But here's the silver lining: investing in employee wellness not only addresses these issues; it can lead to remarkable transformations in workplace culture and output.

To put the data into perspective, let's look at the success story of Google—a company renowned for its innovative approach to employee well-being. In 2012, Google launched a comprehensive wellness program that included fitness initiatives, nutritional guidance, and mental health resources. The results? A staggering 20% increase in overall productivity! The tech giant understood that by fostering a culture of health and well-being, they could unleash the full potential of their workforce. Employees who engaged in regular physical activity reported higher job satisfaction, greater engagement, and a renewed sense of purpose in their roles.

How did Google achieve such impressive results? By prioritizing their employees' physical health, they created an environment that supported well-being at every turn. The wellness program encouraged staff to participate in fitness challenges, take exercise breaks, and access onsite fitness facilities. By making health a fundamental aspect of their corporate culture, Google empowered employees to take charge of their well-being. The outcome was a vibrant, motivated workforce ready to tackle challenges and innovate.

But the story doesn't end there. Organizations across various industries are recognizing that the benefits of prioritizing physical health extend far beyond productivity metrics. The impact on morale, collaboration, and creativity can be transformative. Employees who feel cared for and supported in their physical well-being are more likely to invest in their roles, leading to higher levels of creativity and innovation.

As we delve deeper into the importance of physical health, let's not forget the human element. Each employee brings unique talents, skills, and perspectives to the table, but when physical health falters, so does their ability to contribute effectively. By fostering a culture that prioritizes wellness, companies unlock the potential of their workforce, leading to a happier, healthier, and more engaged team.

So, what can you do to champion physical health within your organization? Start by advocating for wellness programs that cater to the diverse needs of employees. Encourage fitness initiatives, provide access to health resources, and promote a work-life balance that allows employees to recharge. Remember, investing in health is not just a financial decision; it's an investment in the future of your organization.

In the end, the message is clear: your body matters. It's not just about aesthetics or fitness; it's about thriving in your personal and professional life. When physical health is prioritized, everyone wins—employees, employers, and the organization as a whole. So, let's embrace the power of physical well-being, and together, we can create workplaces where everyone can flourish.

After all, a healthy body is the foundation for a thriving career and a fulfilling life!

CHAPTER 4: MAKING TIME FOR EXERCISE

In the hustle and bustle of our modern lives, it often feels like time is our greatest enemy. Meetings pile up, deadlines loom, and personal responsibilities tug at our attention. Amidst this chaos, exercise can easily slip to the bottom of our to-do lists. But what if I told you that making time for exercise is not just possible, but essential for enhancing both your well-being and performance? The key lies in effective time management and smart motivation techniques that allow us to weave physical activity into our daily routines without sacrificing other priorities.

Time Management Strategies

Let's dive into some practical strategies that can help you integrate exercise seamlessly into your day. First up, morning workouts. If you're anything like me, mornings can feel rushed. But consider this: starting your day with a workout can set a positive tone that carries through the rest of your day. It doesn't have to be an hour-long gym session. Even 20 minutes of high-intensity interval training (HIIT) or yoga can kickstart your metabolism and boost your mood.

Tip: Prepare your workout gear the night before and place it near your bed. This way, when your alarm rings, you're greeted by the very thing that will help you power through your day. A quick 20-minute workout can be more invigorating than a cup of coffee!

Next, let's explore the lunch break—often a forgotten opportunity. Instead of scrolling through social media or staring at your screen, how about taking a brisk 15- to 30-minute walk? This not only gets your blood pumping but also clears your mind, enhancing your focus for the remainder of the day. You'll return to your desk recharged and ready to tackle whatever challenges lie ahead.

Tip: Find a walking buddy at work to make it even more enjoyable! You'll benefit from some social interaction while you exercise, creating a win-win situation.

Now, let's talk about those inevitable "lost" hours—like the time spent waiting for meetings to start. Utilize those pockets of time for quick workouts or stretching sessions. Consider doing a few squats or desk push-ups before a meeting. It may sound silly, but those little bursts of activity can contribute significantly to your overall fitness goals.

Motivation Techniques

Once you've identified your time slots for exercise, the next challenge is staying motivated. Setting achievable goals is essential. Instead of aiming for an overwhelming goal like "I want to lose 20 pounds," focus on smaller, manageable objectives. Perhaps aim for a 10-minute walk every day for a week or commit to trying one new workout class. Celebrate these milestones, no matter how small. The sense of accomplishment will fuel your desire to continue.

Consistency is key. Try to incorporate exercise into your routine just like you would with any other commitment. Consider scheduling it in your calendar, treating it as an essential meeting you can't skip. When you treat exercise with the same importance as a work obligation, you're more likely to follow through.

Real-Life Example

Let's take inspiration from Sarah, a successful executive at a leading marketing firm. Sarah's schedule is packed with back-to-back meetings and client calls. But despite her busy lifestyle, she has managed to prioritize her physical health by integrating exercise into her daily routine.

Sarah wakes up at 6:00 AM—not to check emails, but to engage in a quick 30-minute HIIT session at home. "I treat this time as non-negotiable," she says. "It's my time to recharge before the chaos of the day begins." After her workout, she enjoys a healthy breakfast that fuels her for the busy hours ahead.

During her lunch break, instead of staying glued to her desk, she often heads to a nearby park for a brisk walk while catching up with a colleague. "It's amazing how much clearer my mind is after a walk," she shares. "I come back to my desk ready to tackle the next challenge."

Sarah also emphasizes the importance of flexibility. On days when she can't fit in a full workout, she incorporates short, effective bursts of activity. "Even if it's just 10 minutes of stretching or a quick run up the stairs, I find a way to move," she says. This approach not only helps her stay fit but also boosts her mood and productivity.

Conclusion

In a world that often feels overwhelmingly busy, making time for exercise is not just an option—it's a necessity. With effective time management strategies and the right motivation, you can incorporate physical activity into your daily life. Remember, it's about finding what works for you and making it a non-negotiable part of your routine.

So, take a page from Sarah's book. Set achievable goals, create pockets of time for movement, and watch how your physical health transforms not just your body, but your work performance and overall well-being. Embrace the journey of making time for exercise, and you'll discover that investing in your health is the best decision you can make—not just for yourself, but for your career as well!

CHAPTER 5: THE EXERCISE SPECTRUM: FINDING WHAT WORKS

FOR YOU

When it comes to exercise, the choices can feel overwhelming. Should you hit the treadmill, join a yoga class, or lift weights? The truth is, there's no one-size-fits-all approach to physical fitness. Everyone's body, preferences, and goals are unique. This chapter will guide you through the exercise spectrum, exploring different types of activities and helping you discover what works best for you. By choosing exercises that resonate with your interests and lifestyle, you can create a sustainable fitness routine that keeps you motivated and engaged.

Types of Exercise

Let's break down the primary types of exercise and their benefits so you can find your perfect fit:

1. Cardio: Get Your Heart Pumping

Cardiovascular exercise, or cardio, is all about getting your heart rate up and improving your overall cardiovascular health. Activities like running, cycling, swimming, and dancing not only burn calories but also boost your mood through the release of endorphins.

Benefits:

Improves heart and lung health

Increases stamina and endurance

Aids in weight management

Reduces stress and anxiety

If you enjoy rhythm and movement, dance-based workouts like Zumba or hip-hop might be your perfect cardio match.

2. Strength Training: Build Muscle and Confidence

Strength training focuses on building muscle and strength through resistance exercises. Whether it's lifting weights, doing bodyweight exercises, or using resistance bands, this type of training is essential for overall health.

Benefits:

Increases muscle mass and strength

Boosts metabolism and aids in fat loss

Improves bone density

Enhances functional fitness for daily activities

Think about your favorite forms of strength training—whether it's powerlifting, CrossFit, or a simple home workout with resistance bands, the key is to challenge your body in ways that feel rewarding.

3. Flexibility: Stay Agile and Prevent Injury

Flexibility exercises focus on improving the range of motion in your muscles and joints. Activities such as stretching, Pilates, and yoga enhance flexibility, which can prevent injuries and improve posture.

Benefits:

Increases flexibility and mobility

Reduces muscle tension and soreness

Promotes relaxation and stress relief

Enhances overall body awareness

Yoga, in particular, offers a holistic approach that combines flexibility with mindfulness, making it an excellent choice for those seeking mental and physical benefits simultaneously.

4. Mindfulness Practices: The Power of Presence

Mindfulness practices, including yoga and meditation, encourage mental well-being alongside physical fitness. These activities promote self-awareness, reduce stress, and enhance focus.

Benefits:

Decreases stress and anxiety

Improves mental clarity and focus

Fosters emotional resilience

Encourages a deeper connection with your body

Incorporating mindfulness into your routine can be as simple as starting or ending your day with a few minutes of meditation or yoga.

Personal Preferences: Choosing What You Love

Now that you understand the various types of exercise, let's talk about personal preferences. The key to a sustainable fitness routine is finding activities you genuinely enjoy. When exercise feels like a chore, it's easy to lose motivation and abandon your efforts altogether.

Ask yourself: What activities make you feel alive? Do you thrive in a group setting, or do you prefer solitary workouts? Reflecting on your past experiences can help guide your choices.

Group Activities: If you're a social butterfly, group classes or team sports might be your calling. The camaraderie and support of fellow participants can elevate your experience and keep you accountable.

Solo Ventures: If you find solace in solitude, running, hiking, or home workouts might resonate more with you. The peace of mind that comes from engaging in physical activity alone can be a powerful motivator.

Real-Life Example: Finding Joy in Movement

Let's take inspiration from three employees who discovered their preferred forms of exercise, transforming their lives in the process.

Sarah: A graphic designer at a tech firm, Sarah had always been intimidated by the gym. One day, a friend invited her to a dance class. Initially hesitant, she decided to give it a shot. To her surprise, she found herself smiling and laughing throughout the class. "I didn't realize exercise could be so fun!" Sarah exclaimed. She now attends dance classes twice a week and has lost weight while gaining confidence and joy in movement.

David: A project manager who struggled with stress and anxiety, David often found himself working long hours. Realizing he needed to take a break, he joined a local soccer league. "Playing soccer took me back to my childhood," he shared. The thrill of team play and the excitement of the game brought a refreshing sense of joy to his routine. Not only did he build friendships, but he also discovered that the physical activity significantly improved his mood and productivity at work.

Maya: An accountant known for her meticulous attention to detail, Maya felt the effects of sitting all day. Seeking a way to counterbalance her sedentary job, she explored Pilates. The focus on core strength and flexibility not only helped alleviate her back pain but also instilled a sense of mindfulness. "It's like therapy for me," she says, describing her weekly classes as a sanctuary where she reconnects with her body and mind.

Conclusion

Finding your ideal exercise routine is about exploration and discovery. By understanding the different types of exercise and tuning in to what you genuinely enjoy, you can create a sustainable and engaging fitness plan. Remember, the journey to better health doesn't have to be a struggle; it can be a joyful adventure filled with movement, laughter, and community.

So, take the time to explore the exercise spectrum. Try a new class, join a team, or simply dance like no one's watching in your living room. As you embrace activities that bring you joy, you'll find not only improved physical health but also a renewed sense of vitality that spills over into every aspect of your life. Now, go out there and find what moves you!

CHAPTER 6: NUTRITION: FUELING YOUR SUCCESS

In the fast-paced world we live in, where deadlines loom and meetings stack up, the importance of nutrition often gets overshadowed by the hustle and bustle of daily life. However, what you eat is not just about satisfying hunger—it's about fueling your success. Balanced nutrition has a profound impact on your performance, focus, energy, and overall health. In this chapter, we'll explore the nutritional strategies that can elevate your work performance and enhance your well-being, along with practical tips tailored for busy professionals.

Nutritional Impact on Performance

Imagine starting your day with a heavy, greasy breakfast. How does that set the tone for your morning? More often than not, such meals leave you feeling sluggish and unfocused. Conversely, balanced nutrition energizes your body and mind, sharpening your focus and enhancing your productivity.

Here's how nutrition influences your performance:

Enhanced Focus: A well-nourished brain is a focused brain. Nutrients like omega-3 fatty acids (found in fish and nuts) and antioxidants (found in fruits and vegetables) promote cognitive function and mental clarity. When your brain is adequately fueled, you're better equipped to tackle complex tasks and engage in creative problem-solving.

Sustained Energy: Consuming a mix of carbohydrates, proteins, and healthy fats provides a steady release of energy throughout the day. Instead of experiencing peaks and crashes, balanced meals help maintain stable blood sugar levels, allowing for consistent energy and improved concentration.

Overall Health: Nutrition goes hand in hand with your physical health. Proper nutrition reduces the risk of chronic diseases and boosts your immune system, meaning fewer sick days and greater resilience to stress. Healthy employees are happier, more engaged, and more productive.

Healthy Eating Guidelines

Now that we've established the importance of nutrition, let's dive into some practical dietary advice tailored for busy professionals. These guidelines will help you make healthier choices without compromising your time or taste buds:

Start with Breakfast: Never skip breakfast! It kickstarts your metabolism and provides the energy needed to tackle the day. Opt for whole grains, proteins, and healthy fats. Think oatmeal topped with fruits and nuts, or Greek yogurt with granola.

Plan Your Meals: Dedicate a few hours each week to meal prep. Preparing healthy meals in advance saves time and ensures you always have nutritious options on hand. Consider making large batches of soups or salads that you can portion out for the week.

Snack Smart: Keep healthy snacks within reach. Instead of reaching for chips or sugary treats, opt for fruits, nuts, or yogurt. They're not just good for you—they're delicious and easy to grab on the go!

Stay Hydrated: Don't underestimate the power of hydration. Water is essential for maintaining energy levels and concentration. Keep a water bottle at your desk and set reminders to drink throughout the day.

Mindful Eating: Take a moment to enjoy your meals. Eating mindfully—not distracted by screens or work—allows you to savor your food and recognize when you're full, helping prevent overeating.

Real-Life Example: Corporate Chef's Tips for Healthy Snacks

To bring these principles to life, let's hear from Chef Alex Thompson, the head chef at a leading tech company. Alex has been instrumental in transforming the company's approach to nutrition in the workplace, making healthy eating not just accessible but also enjoyable.

1. Vegetable Chips with Hummus: "Instead of traditional potato chips, I recommend making vegetable chips from kale or sweet potatoes. They're baked, not fried, and pack a nutritious punch when paired with hummus. It's a snack that employees rave about!"

2. Energy Bites: "These no-bake energy bites are a hit! Made with oats, nut butter, honey, and dark chocolate chips, they provide a quick burst of energy without the sugar crash. Employees love them because they taste like a treat but are full of goodness!"

3. Fruit Skewers: "For a fun and refreshing snack, we offer fruit skewers. It's easy to grab a skewer with mixed fruits like strawberries, grapes, and pineapple. They're hydrating and loaded with vitamins!"

4. DIY Trail Mix Station: "We set up a trail mix station in the break room, featuring nuts, seeds, dried fruits, and even dark chocolate. Employees love customizing their mixes, and it's a great way to get healthy fats and proteins."

Conclusion

Fueling your body with balanced nutrition is not just a choice; it's a commitment to your well-being and success. By understanding the profound impact nutrition has on performance, you can make informed decisions that enhance your focus, energy, and overall health.

So, as you navigate your busy life, remember: every meal is an opportunity to invest in yourself. Embrace the power of nutrition and let it propel you toward success. With practical strategies, delicious options, and a mindset focused on well-being, you can fuel your journey and unlock your full potential.

Start today—what will you choose for your next meal? The possibilities are endless, and your journey to success begins with the food on your plate!

CHAPTER 7: MEAL PREP FOR BUSY PROFESSIO NALS

In the whirlwind of our daily lives, it often feels like there's barely enough time to breathe, let alone cook a healthy meal. Yet, nourishing our bodies is vital, not just for physical health but for mental clarity and emotional stability. The answer? Meal prep! By mastering meal preparation techniques, you can save time, reduce stress, and fuel your body with nutritious foods —all while enjoying delicious meals that keep you energized throughout the week. Let's dive into the world of meal prep, exploring practical strategies, time-saving tips, and real-life success stories that will inspire you to take control of your eating habits.

Meal Preparation Techniques

Meal prep doesn't have to be an overwhelming task. With the right strategies, you can make it a seamless part of your weekly routine. Here are some effective meal preparation techniques that busy professionals can implement:

Batch Cooking: The cornerstone of meal prep is batch cooking. Dedicate a few hours on the weekend to cook large portions of staple foods like grains, proteins, and vegetables. For instance, prepare a big pot of quinoa, roast a tray of seasonal vegetables, and grill chicken or tofu. Store these components in individual containers, and mix and match them throughout the week for quick, nutritious meals.

Quick, Nutritious Recipes: Aim for recipes that require minimal prep time but pack a nutritional punch. Consider dishes like stir-fries, salads, and casseroles. A simple stir-fry can come together in 15 minutes, using pre-chopped vegetables and a lean protein source. Keep an arsenal of go-to recipes that can be adapted based on what you have on hand.

Use Freezer-Friendly Meals: Some meals freeze beautifully, making them perfect for those particularly hectic weeks. Soups, stews, and chili are excellent options that can be portioned out and stored for later. Simply thaw and reheat when you need a nutritious meal in a pinch.

Time-Saving Tips

Efficiency is key when it comes to meal prep. Here are some time-saving tips to streamline your grocery shopping and meal planning:

Create a Meal Plan: Spend a few minutes each week mapping out your meals. This not only helps you stay organized but also ensures you have everything you need when you go shopping. Aim for a mix of proteins, whole grains, and colorful vegetables to keep your meals varied and exciting.

Make a Shopping List: Once your meal plan is set, create a detailed shopping list organized by categories (produce, proteins, grains, etc.). This will save you time in the grocery store and prevent impulse purchases. Stick to the list, and you'll be in and out in no time!

Choose Convenient Grocery Options: Consider using grocery delivery services or curbside pickup to save time. Many grocery stores offer pre-chopped vegetables and ready-to-cook meal kits that can simplify your prep process. While these options may cost a bit more, the time you save can be invaluable.

Keep it Simple: Remember, meal prep doesn't have to be elaborate. Focus on simple, nourishing meals that you enjoy. It's better to have a few easy go-to meals than to overwhelm yourself with complex recipes that you won't stick to.

Real-Life Example: A Working Parent's Success Story

To illustrate the power of meal prep, let's meet Sarah Thompson, a dedicated working parent who has mastered the art of meal preparation. Juggling a demanding job and her two young children, Sarah realized that her family's eating habits were suffering. They often resorted to fast food or unhealthy snacks when life got busy. Determined to change this pattern, Sarah implemented a weekly meal prep routine that transformed their approach to eating.

Sarah's Weekly Meal Prep Routine:

Sunday Prep Day: Every Sunday, Sarah sets aside a couple of hours to prepare meals for the week. She cooks large portions of brown rice, quinoa, and roasted vegetables. She also grills chicken breasts and prepares a big batch of lentil soup.

Family Involvement: To make it a fun family activity, Sarah involves her children in the process. They help wash and chop vegetables, which not only teaches them about healthy eating but also creates lasting memories in the kitchen.

Easy Grab-and-Go Options: Sarah makes sure to have healthy snacks on hand, like sliced veggies, hummus, and homemade energy bars. She also prepares easy breakfast options, such as overnight oats, so the family can grab them on busy mornings.

Meal Variety: With her batch-cooked ingredients, Sarah creates a variety of meals throughout the week. One night, they enjoy stir-fried quinoa with vegetables and grilled chicken; another night, it's lentil soup with whole-grain bread. The possibilities are endless!

Since implementing this routine, Sarah has noticed a significant improvement in her family's health and well-being. They are eating more nutritious meals, spending less money on takeout, and enjoying family time in the kitchen. "Meal prep has changed our lives," Sarah shares. "We're healthier, happier, and it's so much easier to stay on track with our eating habits."

Conclusion

Meal preparation is a powerful tool for busy professionals seeking to prioritize their health and well-being. By adopting simple strategies and incorporating time-saving tips, you can transform your relationship with food and ensure you're fueling your body with nourishing meals.

Remember, meal prep isn't about perfection; it's about creating a sustainable routine that fits your lifestyle. Whether you're cooking for yourself or a busy family, the key is to find what works for you and embrace the journey. With a little planning and creativity, you can take control of your meals, save time, and ultimately fuel your success—one delicious bite at a time. So grab those containers, set aside some time, and get ready to make meal prep a game changer in your life!

CHAPTER 8: STAYING HYDRATED: THE POWER OF WATER

Imagine this: you wake up in the morning, ready to take on the day, but instead of feeling energized, you feel sluggish and unfocused. You might blame it on a lack of sleep or the stress of a busy schedule, but one critical factor could be at play: hydration. Water is not just a thirst-quencher; it's a vital component of your overall well-being, profoundly influencing your cognitive and physical performance. In this chapter, we'll explore the incredible power of hydration, practical guidelines for ensuring you drink enough water, and how even the busiest professionals can integrate effective hydration strategies into their daily lives.

Hydration and Productivity

It's easy to underestimate the impact of hydration on our performance, but studies show that even mild dehydration can have significant cognitive and physical effects. Just a 2% drop in body water can lead to decreased concentration, fatigue, and headaches. This means that if you're feeling distracted or sluggish at work, it might not just be the workload—it could be your water intake!

Research highlights the following effects of dehydration:

Cognitive Decline: When you're dehydrated, your brain struggles to function optimally. Studies indicate that dehydration can lead to impaired attention, reduced memory performance, and decreased alertness. It's no wonder that when you feel parched, your ability to think clearly and make decisions can plummet.

Physical Performance: Dehydration doesn't just affect your mind; it impacts your body too. Lack of adequate hydration can lead to reduced endurance, muscle fatigue, and increased risk of injury. Whether you're hitting the gym or simply tackling your to-do list, staying hydrated is crucial for maintaining your energy levels.

Mood and Well-Being: Ever noticed that you feel irritable when you haven't had enough water? Research supports this; dehydration can lead to increased feelings of anxiety and fatigue. By prioritizing hydration, you can improve your mood and overall emotional well-being, making it easier to tackle challenges with a positive attitude.

Guidelines for Hydration

So, how much water should you be drinking daily to ensure optimal hydration? While the general guideline of eight 8-ounce glasses (about 2 liters) is a great start, individual needs vary based on factors like age, weight, activity level, and climate. Here are some practical recommendations to help you stay on track:

Listen to Your Body: Thirst is a natural indicator that your body needs water. Pay attention to your thirst cues and drink when you feel dry or parched.

Set Daily Goals: Aim to drink a specific amount of water throughout the day. A common target is to consume half your body weight in ounces. For example, if you weigh 160 pounds, aim for about 80 ounces of water daily.

Hydration at Work: Keep a water bottle at your desk to remind you to sip throughout the day. Refill it regularly and set hourly goals to ensure you're meeting your hydration targets.

Incorporate Hydrating Foods: Remember that fruits and vegetables also contribute to your hydration. Foods like cucumbers, watermelon, and oranges are not only delicious but also packed with water, helping you stay hydrated in a tasty way.

Make it a Habit: Establish a routine that incorporates water consumption. Start your day with a glass of water, drink before each meal, and keep track of your intake throughout the day. The more consistent you are, the more natural it will become.

Real-Life Example: An Athlete's Hydration Strategy

To illustrate the power of hydration, let's take a closer look at the hydration strategy of Sarah Johnson, a competitive marathon runner. Sarah understands that staying properly hydrated is critical for her performance, especially during grueling training sessions and races. Here's how she maximizes her hydration to optimize her performance:

Pre-Training Hydration: Before any training session, Sarah ensures she drinks at least 16 ounces of water. This helps her start her workout well-hydrated, improving her stamina and focus.

During Training: Sarah carries a water bottle with her during runs, aiming to drink at least 8 ounces every 30 minutes. For longer sessions, she incorporates electrolyte drinks to replenish lost minerals.

Post-Training Recovery: After a workout, Sarah immediately rehydrates with a combination of water and a recovery drink that contains electrolytes and carbohydrates. This aids her muscle recovery and helps her avoid dehydration.

Daily Routine: Outside of training, Sarah maintains her hydration by setting reminders on her phone to drink water every hour. She tracks her daily intake using an app to ensure she meets her hydration goals.

Practical Tips for Office Workers

While Sarah's strategy is geared toward athletes, busy professionals can adopt similar hydration habits. Here are some practical tips:

Use a Reusable Water Bottle: Invest in a stylish reusable water bottle that you can carry around. This not only serves as a reminder to drink more but also reduces plastic waste.

Hydration Apps: Download a hydration app to track your water intake and set reminders throughout the day. Many apps allow you to log the beverages you consume, helping you stay accountable.

Infuse Your Water: If plain water bores you, try infusing it with fruits, herbs, or even vegetables. A splash of lemon or a handful of berries can turn your water into a refreshing treat that encourages you to drink more.

Buddy System: Partner up with a colleague to support each other in staying hydrated. Share your daily goals and check in with each other to celebrate your progress.

Conclusion

Staying hydrated is a simple yet powerful way to enhance your overall well-being, productivity, and performance. As you embark on this journey, remember that hydration is not just a one-time effort but a daily commitment. By implementing these practical strategies, you can transform your relationship with water and harness its incredible benefits.

So, raise your water bottle and toast to your health! With every sip, you're fueling your mind and body, paving the way for success in every endeavor. Embrace the power of hydration, and watch as your energy levels soar, your mood improves, and your productivity reaches new heights. It's time to make hydration a priority and experience the difference it can make in your life!

CHAPTER 9: SLEEP: YOUR SECRET WEAPON

In our fast-paced, always-on world, the value of sleep is often overshadowed by the hustle culture that glorifies late nights and early mornings. But what if I told you that the real secret weapon for productivity and success lies in the quality of your sleep? That's right! Prioritizing sleep can transform not only your health but also your performance at work and in life. In this chapter, we'll explore why quality sleep is essential, dive into the science behind sleep cycles, and share an inspiring real-life journey of an entrepreneur who harnessed the power of sleep to elevate his game.

Importance of Quality Sleep

Imagine waking up each morning feeling refreshed, energized, and ready to tackle the day. That's the magic of quality sleep! Sleep is not just a time for rest; it's a crucial period for your body and mind to recharge, repair, and rejuvenate. Here's how it affects your concentration, memory, and overall productivity:

Enhanced Concentration: When you sleep well, your brain performs at its peak. Quality sleep allows your mind to clear out the clutter and consolidate information from the previous day, leading to improved focus and attention during waking hours. Conversely, inadequate sleep can lead to foggy thinking and difficulty concentrating, making even simple tasks feel overwhelming.

Improved Memory: Sleep plays a vital role in memory consolidation. During deep sleep, your brain processes and stores information, creating connections that help you recall facts and skills later. Lack of sleep disrupts this process, leading to forgetfulness and decreased learning capacity.

Boosted Productivity: Studies show that individuals who prioritize sleep report higher productivity levels. A well-rested mind is more creative, solution-oriented, and efficient. On the flip side, sleep deprivation is linked to increased errors, slower reaction times, and decreased motivation. It's clear: to perform at your best, you must prioritize your nightly rest.

Sleep Science

To truly appreciate the significance of sleep, let's delve into the science of sleep cycles. Sleep is not a monolithic state; it consists of several cycles that alternate between REM (Rapid Eye Movement) and non-REM sleep. Each cycle lasts about 90 minutes and repeats several times throughout the night. Here's a breakdown:

Non-REM Sleep: This stage includes three phases: light sleep, moderate sleep, and deep sleep. Deep sleep is particularly crucial as it's when your body performs essential functions like tissue repair, muscle growth, and immune system strengthening.

REM Sleep: This phase is where dreaming occurs, and it plays a significant role in emotional regulation, creativity, and problem-solving. During REM sleep, the brain is highly active, processing emotions and experiences from the day.

Impact of Sleep Deprivation: Lack of sleep can disrupt these cycles, leading to an overall decline in cognitive and physical health. Research indicates that just one night of poor sleep can impair attention, alertness, concentration, reasoning, and problem-solving skills. Prolonged sleep deprivation can lead to serious health issues, including anxiety, depression, and cardiovascular problems.

Real-Life Example: An Entrepreneur's Journey to Better Sleep Habits

Meet David, a successful entrepreneur whose initial relationship with sleep was one of neglect. In the early years of his startup, he prided himself on working long hours, believing that sacrificing sleep was a necessary trade-off for success. But as his business grew, he began to notice the detrimental effects of his sleepless nights: diminished creativity, increased irritability, and a constant feeling of being overwhelmed.

Recognizing that something needed to change, David embarked on a journey to improve his sleep habits. Here's how he transformed his routine and environment:

Setting a Sleep Schedule: David committed to a consistent sleep schedule, going to bed and waking up at the same time every day, even on weekends. This practice helped regulate his body's internal clock, making it easier to fall asleep and wake up feeling refreshed.

Creating a Sleep-Friendly Environment: He revamped his bedroom to promote better sleep. David invested in blackout curtains, a comfortable mattress, and eliminated any disruptive noises. He also minimized screen time before bed, opting instead for relaxing activities like reading or meditating.

Mindfulness and Relaxation Techniques: To ease his mind after a busy day, David incorporated mindfulness practices into his routine. He began meditating and practicing deep-breathing exercises, allowing him to unwind and clear his mind before sleep.

Monitoring Sleep Quality: David started using a sleep-tracking app to monitor his sleep patterns. By analyzing his sleep data, he identified habits that hindered his rest and made adjustments accordingly. This self-awareness proved invaluable in his journey toward better sleep.

The results were astounding. Within weeks, David noticed a dramatic improvement in his focus and creativity. He felt more energized and motivated, which translated into increased productivity at work. His decision-making abilities sharpened, and he could tackle challenges with renewed vigor. Most importantly, he rediscovered a sense of balance in his life, realizing that prioritizing sleep was not a weakness but a strength.

Conclusion

Sleep is your secret weapon—an often-overlooked key

to unlocking your potential and achieving success. By understanding the importance of quality sleep and the science behind it, you can harness its power to enhance your concentration, memory, and overall productivity.

As you embark on your journey to better sleep habits, take inspiration from David's story. Remember that prioritizing sleep is not just about getting more hours; it's about cultivating a healthy relationship with rest. By implementing consistent routines, creating a sleep-friendly environment, and embracing relaxation techniques, you too can unlock the transformative power of quality sleep.

So, let's raise a toast (preferably with a calming herbal tea) to better sleep and the endless possibilities it brings! With every restful night, you're fueling your potential and setting the stage for a vibrant, successful life. Embrace your sleep as the powerful tool it is, and watch as it propels you toward your goals and aspirations!

CHAPTER 10: CREATING A SLEEP SANCTUARY

In our quest for success and well-being, the space where we rest can make all the difference. The bedroom is more than just a room; it's a sanctuary—a sacred space where you can recharge, dream, and prepare for the challenges of a new day. In this chapter, we'll explore how to design a sleep-friendly environment, develop a soothing bedtime routine, and share insights from a sleep expert who has helped countless individuals transform their sleep settings. Get ready to create your personal sleep sanctuary and unlock the power of restful nights!

Designing Sleep-Friendly Spaces

The first step to creating a sleep sanctuary is optimizing your bedroom environment. A few key factors can significantly influence your ability to drift off into a deep, restorative slumber.

Lighting: Light is one of the most powerful regulators of your sleep-wake cycle. Aim for a dim, cozy atmosphere in the evening to signal to your body that it's time to wind down. Consider using soft, warm lighting, such as lamps with yellow-toned bulbs or adjustable dimmers. Blackout curtains can also work wonders, blocking out any disruptive streetlights or morning sun, allowing you to wake up refreshed.

Temperature: The ideal sleep temperature is typically between 60 and 67 degrees Fahrenheit (15 to 19 degrees Celsius). A cooler room promotes better sleep, as your body naturally cools down during the night. Invest in a good-quality thermostat or use fans to regulate airflow. Consider breathable bedding materials, such as cotton or linen, which help maintain a comfortable temperature throughout the night.

Noise Control: Noise can be a major disruptor of sleep quality. If you live in a noisy environment, consider using white noise machines or soothing sound apps that play nature sounds or gentle music to mask disruptive sounds. Earplugs can also be effective for blocking out noise, ensuring you stay in the peaceful bubble of your sleep sanctuary.

Declutter and Organize: A clutter-free environment promotes a sense of calm and tranquility. Take some time to organize your space, removing any distractions or items that don't belong. Consider a minimalist approach, where you keep only the essentials that bring you joy and peace. A tidy room can help create a clear mind, making it easier to relax and fall asleep.

Routine Development

Now that you've optimized your sleep space, let's talk about the importance of a bedtime routine. Establishing a consistent winding-down ritual is key to signaling to your body that it's time to transition from the hustle and bustle of the day to the calm of the night.

Set a Consistent Bedtime: Choose a bedtime that allows for adequate rest and stick to it as closely as possible, even on weekends. Consistency helps regulate your body's internal clock, making it easier to fall asleep and wake up at the desired times.

Wind Down with Intention: About an hour before bed, begin your winding-down process. Engage in calming activities that help you relax and disconnect from the day. This could include reading a book, practicing gentle yoga, or taking a warm bath. Dimming the lights during this time can also help cue your body that it's time to relax.

Limit Screen Time: The blue light emitted from screens can disrupt your body's production of melatonin, the hormone that regulates sleep. Aim to unplug from devices at least 30 minutes before bed. Instead of scrolling through your phone or watching TV, opt for activities that promote relaxation and prepare your mind for sleep.

Practice Gratitude: Incorporating a gratitude practice into your bedtime routine can help shift your focus from stress to positivity. Spend a few minutes reflecting on the things you are grateful for, writing them down in a journal. This practice not only helps you unwind but also fosters a positive mindset for the day ahead.

Real-Life Example: Insights from a Sleep Expert

To gain deeper insights into creating the ultimate sleep sanctuary, we spoke with Dr. Sarah Mitchell, a leading sleep expert known for her transformative sleep consultations. Dr. Mitchell has worked with clients from all walks of life, helping them optimize their sleep environments and routines. Here's what she shared:

Before and After Transformations:

Before: One of her clients, Laura, struggled with insomnia due to her cluttered, brightly lit bedroom filled with gadgets and distractions. Laura often found herself tossing and turning, unable to relax and fall asleep.

After: With Dr. Mitchell's guidance, Laura transformed her bedroom into a serene sleep sanctuary. She decluttered her space, painted the walls a soothing blue, and installed blackout curtains. Laura replaced her bright overhead lights with soft bedside lamps and implemented a calming bedtime routine. The results were remarkable: within weeks, Laura reported falling asleep within minutes and enjoying uninterrupted nights of rest.

Dr. Mitchell emphasizes that small changes can lead to significant improvements in sleep quality. She encourages individuals to take time to explore what works best for them, reminding us that each person's sleep sanctuary will look different.

Conclusion

Creating a sleep sanctuary is an essential step in prioritizing your health and well-being. By optimizing your sleep environment and developing a soothing bedtime routine, you can cultivate a space that promotes restorative sleep and enhances your overall quality of life.

Take a moment to reflect on your own sleep space. What small changes can you make today to transform it into your personal sanctuary? Whether it's adjusting the lighting, decluttering, or committing to a calming bedtime routine, each step you take brings you closer to unlocking the rejuvenating power of restful sleep.

Remember, a well-rested mind and body are your greatest allies in achieving your goals and living a vibrant life. Embrace the journey of creating your sleep sanctuary, and watch as your nights transform into a source of strength and inspiration. The power to rest, recharge, and thrive is within your reach—let your sleep sanctuary be the foundation of your success!

CHAPTER 11: BALANCING WORK AND LIFE

In the fast-paced world we live in, achieving a harmonious work-life balance feels like an elusive dream for many. The demands of work often bleed into our personal lives, leaving us feeling overwhelmed and drained. Yet, finding this balance is not only essential for our mental and emotional well-being; it's also key to our productivity and overall success. In this chapter, we will explore effective strategies for establishing boundaries, prioritizing tasks, and creating a fulfilling life that encompasses both work and play. Get ready to reclaim your time and enhance your life!

Work-Life Balance Strategies

The first step toward achieving work-life balance is to establish clear boundaries between your professional and personal lives. This isn't just about clocking out at the end of the day; it's about creating a mindset that values both aspects equally.

Set Clear Boundaries: It's crucial to define what work means to you and when you'll engage in it. Communicate these boundaries to your colleagues and family members. For instance, if you decide that evenings are family time, turn off work notifications and focus on nurturing those relationships. This intentional separation allows you to recharge and gives your mind the space to unwind.

Create a Dedicated Workspace: If you're working from home, designate a specific area as your workspace. This physical separation reinforces your mental boundaries. When you're in this space, you're in "work mode," and when you step away, you transition to "home mode." This simple change can significantly impact your productivity and overall satisfaction.

Learn to Say No: Saying yes to every request can lead to burnout and resentment. Practice assertiveness by evaluating what truly aligns with your goals and values before committing to new tasks or projects. Remember, it's okay to prioritize your well-being over obligations that don't serve you.

Time Allocation Techniques

Time is one of our most valuable resources, and how we allocate it can greatly affect our work-life balance. Here are some practical techniques to help you prioritize tasks and set realistic expectations:

Prioritize Your Tasks: Use the Eisenhower Matrix—a tool that categorizes tasks into four quadrants based on urgency and importance. Focus on what's truly important and urgent while learning to delegate or postpone less critical tasks. This strategy helps streamline your workload and reduces overwhelm.

Set Realistic Expectations: Avoid the trap of perfectionism by setting achievable goals. Break larger tasks into smaller, manageable steps. Celebrate your progress along the way rather than waiting for a grand finale. This approach not only keeps you motivated but also allows for flexibility in your schedule.

Embrace the Power of Time Blocking: Allocate specific time slots in your calendar for different tasks. This technique allows you to stay focused and minimizes distractions. For instance, dedicate certain hours of the day for deep work, meetings, and personal time. Having a structured schedule can create a sense of accomplishment and purpose.

Real-Life Example: A Case Study

To illustrate the transformative power of work-life balance, let's take a closer look at a company that has embraced flexible work policies and reaped the rewards—Acme Innovations. This mid-sized tech company recognized early on that its employees were struggling to maintain a healthy work-life balance, leading to high turnover rates and low morale.

Implementation of Flexible Work Policies: In response, Acme Innovations implemented flexible work policies that allowed employees to set their schedules, work remotely when needed, and take mental health days without stigma. They encouraged open conversations about workload and mental health, creating a culture of support and understanding.

Results: The impact was remarkable. Within six months, employee satisfaction scores skyrocketed by 35%, and productivity increased by 20%. Team members reported feeling more engaged and less stressed, leading to improved creativity and collaboration. Acme Innovations demonstrated that when employees feel valued and supported, they are more likely to contribute positively to the organization.

Employee Testimonials: Employees shared their stories of transformation. Sarah, a project manager, noted, "With the flexibility to work from home when needed, I've been able to manage my family obligations without sacrificing my career. I feel empowered and more focused."

Another employee, Jason, said, "Having the option to adjust my schedule means I can work when I'm most productive. I'm no longer juggling late-night work and early-morning family commitments."

Conclusion

Balancing work and life is not just a goal; it's a necessity for a fulfilling and productive existence. By establishing boundaries, prioritizing tasks, and learning from successful companies like Acme Innovations, you can reclaim your time and create a life that embraces both professional success and personal joy.

As you embark on this journey toward a healthier work-life balance, take a moment to reflect on your current situation. What boundaries can you set today? What tasks can you prioritize to lighten your load? Remember, achieving balance is an ongoing process, and every small step counts.

You have the power to shape your work-life balance, fostering an environment that supports your well-being. Embrace the strategies shared in this chapter and watch as your productivity, satisfaction, and happiness soar. The path to a fulfilling life starts with you—let's take that first step together!

CHAPTER 12: THE ROLE OF BREAKS IN ENHANCING FOCUS

In the relentless pursuit of productivity, many of us overlook one crucial element that can supercharge our efficiency and creativity: breaks. Yes, you heard that right! Taking regular breaks is not just an indulgence; it's a powerful strategy for enhancing focus and achieving peak performance. In this chapter, we will explore the myriad benefits of breaks, practical techniques for effective downtime, and a real-life success story that demonstrates the impact of implementing a break policy in the workplace. Get ready to unlock the potential of taking a step back to leap forward!

Benefits of Regular Breaks

Imagine this: You're deep in concentration, fully immersed in a project when suddenly, your focus begins to wane. Your thoughts become muddled, and your creativity stagnates. Instead of pushing through the mental fog, what if you took a brief pause? Research shows that regular breaks can significantly enhance focus, creativity, and overall productivity. Here's why:

Improved Concentration: Our brains are not designed for marathon focus sessions. Studies have shown that after about 25 to 30 minutes of concentrated work, cognitive fatigue sets in. Taking short breaks helps reset your brain, allowing you to return with renewed energy and sharper focus.

Increased Creativity: Breaks encourage divergent thinking—where your mind explores new ideas and connections. By stepping away from a task, you give your subconscious the opportunity to process information, often leading to breakthroughs and innovative solutions.

Enhanced Well-Being: Regular breaks reduce stress and prevent burnout. When you prioritize downtime, you cultivate a healthier work environment that supports emotional and mental well-being. A well-rested mind is a powerful asset!

Techniques for Effective Breaks

Now that we understand the importance of breaks, how can we

make the most of them? Here are some effective techniques to transform your downtime into productive moments:

The Pomodoro Technique: This popular time management method encourages you to work for 25 minutes and then take a 5-minute break. After completing four cycles, take a longer break of 15-30 minutes. Use this time to stretch, hydrate, or practice mindfulness.

Nature Walks: A brief walk in nature can do wonders for your mind. Studies have shown that spending time outdoors reduces stress and enhances cognitive function. So, when you need a break, step outside, breathe in the fresh air, and let nature rejuvenate your spirit.

Mindful Breathing: Take a few minutes to practice deep breathing exercises. Close your eyes, inhale deeply through your nose, hold for a moment, and exhale slowly through your mouth. This simple technique helps calm your mind, reduces anxiety, and enhances focus.

Creative Hobbies: Engage in a quick, enjoyable activity that sparks joy—whether it's doodling, playing a musical instrument, or solving a puzzle. These activities activate different parts of your brain, boosting creativity and problem-solving skills.

Real-Life Example: A Success Story

Let's delve into a real-life example that highlights the transformative power of break policies: Tech Innovations Inc., a rapidly growing tech company. Faced with high stress levels and declining productivity among its employees, the leadership team knew it had to make a change.

Implementation of Break Policy: After researching the benefits of breaks, Tech Innovations Inc. implemented a structured break policy. They encouraged employees to take regular, scheduled breaks throughout the day. The company even created comfortable relaxation areas equipped with games, plants, and cozy seating to promote rejuvenation.

Results: The outcome was nothing short of remarkable. Within three months, employee satisfaction scores surged by 40%. Productivity increased by an impressive 25%, with teams reporting higher levels of creativity and collaboration.

Employee Testimonials: Employees shared their experiences of how breaks transformed their workday. Mark, a software developer, said, "I used to feel guilty taking breaks, but now I embrace them. The short walks and relaxed chats with colleagues have made a world of difference. I'm more focused and have so many more creative ideas!"

Sarah, a project manager, added, "The relaxation area has become my go-to spot. Just stepping away for a few minutes allows me to return to my tasks with fresh energy and clarity."

Conclusion

In a world that often equates busyness with productivity, it's essential to recognize that taking breaks is a powerful tool for enhancing focus and performance. By understanding the benefits of regular breaks and incorporating effective techniques into your daily routine, you can unlock a new level of creativity, productivity, and well-being.

As you reflect on your work habits, ask yourself: How can I prioritize breaks in my day? What techniques resonate with me? Remember, taking time to recharge is not a luxury; it's a necessity. Embrace the role of breaks in your life, and watch as your focus and productivity soar to new heights.

Let's take that first step together—pause, breathe, and empower yourself to achieve greatness through the art of taking breaks!

CHAPTER 13: STRETCH IT OUT: THE POWER OF MOVEMENT

In today's fast-paced work environment, where deadlines loom and tasks pile up, many of us find ourselves glued to our desks for hours on end. We power through meetings, emails, and projects, often ignoring the subtle cues our bodies send us. But here's a game-changing truth: movement is not just beneficial—it's essential! In this chapter, we will explore the incredible benefits of stretching and movement breaks, provide simple techniques you can incorporate into your workday, and showcase a real-life example of an office culture that has embraced this philosophy. Get ready to stretch your way to a more energized, focused, and productive you!

Benefits of Stretching

Have you ever noticed that after sitting for extended periods, your body feels stiff and your mind sluggish? This is where the power of movement comes into play. Incorporating stretching and movement breaks into your routine offers a multitude of benefits:

Reduced Physical Tension: Sitting for long periods can lead to muscle tightness, particularly in the neck, shoulders, and back. Stretching helps alleviate this tension, improving overall comfort and mobility. By regularly stretching, you can enhance your body's flexibility and prevent those pesky aches and pains that come from prolonged sitting.

Enhanced Mental Clarity: Just as physical tension can cloud your mind, mental fatigue can hamper your productivity. Movement breaks, especially those that include stretching, stimulate blood flow and oxygenate the brain, resulting in improved concentration and cognitive function. You'll find yourself returning to your tasks with renewed clarity and creativity.

Boosted Mood and Energy: Physical activity, even in small doses, triggers the release of endorphins—those feel-good hormones that lift your mood and increase your energy levels. Taking a few moments to stretch can help shake off lethargy and reinvigorate your spirits, making you feel more engaged and motivated.

Stretching Techniques

Now that we understand the importance of stretching, let's explore some simple stretches you can easily incorporate into your workday, even at your desk. These movements require minimal space and can be performed in just a few minutes:

Neck Rolls: To relieve tension in your neck, sit up straight and gently roll your head in a circular motion, first clockwise and then counterclockwise. Repeat for 30 seconds in each direction. This stretch helps ease stiffness and promotes relaxation.

Shoulder Shrugs: Raise your shoulders towards your ears in a shrug, hold for a moment, and then release them down. Repeat this 10 times to relieve tension in your shoulders and upper back. It's a quick way to reset your posture!

Seated Torso Twist: While sitting, place your right hand on the back of your chair and twist your torso to the right, holding for 15-30 seconds. Repeat on the left side. This stretch enhances spinal mobility and helps alleviate lower back tension.

Wrist and Finger Stretch: Stretch out your wrists and fingers by extending one arm in front of you, palm facing up. With your other hand, gently pull back on your fingers, holding for 15 seconds. This stretch is especially beneficial for those who spend a lot of time typing.

Chair Pose: Stand up and, using your chair for balance, lift one leg behind you and bend at the knee, holding it with your hand. Hold for 15 seconds, then switch legs. This stretch engages your core and improves balance.

Real-Life Example: The Stretch Break Culture at HappyCorp

To illustrate the transformative power of stretching and movement breaks, let's look at HappyCorp, a company renowned for its innovative approach to employee well-being. Faced with a growing concern over employee burnout and disengagement, the leadership team decided to take action.

Implementation of Stretch Breaks: They introduced a dedicated "Stretch It Out" program, encouraging employees to take 5-minute stretching breaks every hour. The company equipped break areas with yoga mats and guided stretching sessions led by trained staff. They even created a "Stretch Buddy" system, pairing employees to motivate one another to participate.

Results: The results were astounding. Employee feedback indicated a significant reduction in physical discomfort, with 75% reporting fewer headaches and back pains after just a few weeks. Productivity soared by 20%, with teams collaborating more effectively and creatively.

Employee Testimonials: Sarah, a marketing specialist, shared, "At first, I was skeptical about taking breaks for stretching, but now I can't imagine my day without it! I feel so much more energized and focused after a quick stretch."

James, a software engineer, added, "The stretch breaks have transformed our office culture. We're more connected, and it feels good to support one another's well-being."

Conclusion

Incorporating movement breaks and stretching into your daily routine is a simple yet powerful strategy for enhancing your physical and mental well-being. By embracing the benefits of movement, you can reduce tension, boost productivity, and cultivate a more positive work environment.

As you reflect on your daily habits, ask yourself: How can I prioritize movement and stretching in my routine? What stretches resonate with me? Remember, taking time to stretch and move is not just a break from work; it's an investment in your health and productivity.

So, let's stretch it out together! Stand up, take a deep breath, and feel the energy flow through you. Embrace the power of movement, and watch as it transforms your workday for the better!

CHAPTER 14: MENTAL WELLNESS AND PHYSICAL HEALTH

In our quest for a fulfilling life, we often overlook a vital truth: mental wellness and physical health are not just linked—they are inextricably intertwined. Picture this: you wake up feeling energized, your mind sharp, and ready to tackle the day ahead. But what happens when stress creeps in, or your body starts to feel worn down? The truth is, when we neglect one aspect of our health, the other often suffers. In this chapter, we will explore the profound interconnectedness of mental wellness and physical health, delve into mindfulness techniques that can seamlessly fit into your daily routine, and share inspiring real-life stories of employees who have harnessed these practices to boost their job performance. Get ready to discover how nurturing both your mind and body can lead to a more vibrant, productive, and balanced life!

Interconnectedness of Wellness

Imagine your body and mind as two sides of the same coin. When one thrives, the other flourishes, but when one falters, the other can spiral downwards. Scientific research supports this synergy, showing that our mental state profoundly influences our physical health, and vice versa.

The Physical Impact of Mental Health: Chronic stress, anxiety, and depression can manifest physically, leading to fatigue, muscle tension, and a weakened immune system. According to the World Health Organization, mental health issues are often linked to physical health conditions like heart disease, diabetes, and obesity. When we neglect our mental wellness, we inadvertently jeopardize our physical health.

The Mental Impact of Physical Health: Conversely, our physical health directly affects our mental state. Regular physical activity releases endorphins—natural mood lifters that can combat feelings of stress and anxiety. A study published in the Journal of Health Psychology found that individuals who engage in regular exercise report higher levels of well-being and lower levels of stress. By prioritizing physical health, we can create a solid foundation for a resilient mind.

Mindfulness Techniques

So, how do we cultivate a harmonious relationship between mental wellness and physical health? Enter mindfulness. This powerful practice encourages us to stay present, fostering awareness of our thoughts and feelings without judgment. Here are some practical mindfulness techniques you can integrate into your daily routine:

Mindful Breathing: Start your day with just five minutes of mindful breathing. Find a comfortable seated position, close your eyes, and focus on your breath. Inhale deeply through your nose, hold for a moment, and exhale slowly through your mouth. This practice calms the mind, reduces anxiety, and sets a positive tone for the day ahead.

Body Scan: Take a few minutes each day to perform a body scan. Lie down comfortably and mentally scan your body from head to toe, paying attention to any areas of tension or discomfort. Acknowledge these feelings without judgment, then consciously relax each muscle group. This technique enhances body awareness and promotes relaxation.

Mindful Movement: Incorporate mindfulness into your physical activity. Whether you're running, practicing yoga, or walking, focus on how your body feels with each movement. Be present in the moment, savoring the sensations of strength, flexibility, and vitality. This practice not only enhances your workout but also enriches your mental state.

Gratitude Journaling: Set aside a few minutes each evening to write down three things you're grateful for. This simple yet powerful practice can shift your focus from stress to positivity, fostering a mindset of abundance and appreciation.

Real-Life Example: The Power of Mindfulness and Exercise at BrightTech

To illustrate the transformative impact of combining mindfulness and physical activity, let's explore the experience of BrightTech, a thriving tech company that has prioritized mental wellness alongside physical health.

Integrating Mindfulness and Exercise: Recognizing the importance of employee well-being, BrightTech introduced a unique program called "Mindful Motion." This initiative encouraged employees to participate in weekly mindfulness workshops, followed by group exercise sessions such as yoga and tai chi. The goal was simple: to cultivate a culture of awareness, resilience, and physical vitality.

The Results: Employees embraced this initiative wholeheartedly. Mary, a software developer, shared, "At first, I thought it was just another wellness program. But after attending the mindfulness sessions, I realized how much my stress affected my work. I started practicing mindfulness every morning, and now, I feel more focused and less overwhelmed during busy times."

James, a project manager, experienced a similar transformation. "The combination of mindfulness and exercise has been a game-changer for me. I've noticed a significant boost in my productivity, and I'm more engaged with my team. Plus, I feel healthier than ever!"

The Impact on Job Performance: BrightTech reported a remarkable 25% increase in overall employee satisfaction and a 30% reduction in stress-related absenteeism after implementing the Mindful Motion program. Employees felt more connected to their work and each other, and the office culture shifted toward one of support and understanding.

Conclusion

Mental wellness and physical health are deeply interconnected, influencing every aspect of our lives. By integrating mindfulness practices into our daily routines, we can create a harmonious balance that enhances our overall well-being. Remember, nurturing your mind and body isn't just an individual pursuit— it's a collective journey that benefits not only you but also your workplace and community.

As you move forward, consider the ways you can incorporate mindfulness and movement into your life. Start small—perhaps with mindful breathing or a short stretching session. As you begin to experience the benefits, you'll find yourself more resilient, focused, and energized.

So, let's embrace this journey together! Your well-being awaits— unlock the power of mindfulness and physical health, and watch as it transforms your life for the better!

CHAPTER 15: THE OFFICE ERGONOMICS REVOLUTION

Welcome to the revolution—an office transformation that prioritizes not just productivity, but the well-being of every employee! In an era where we spend countless hours glued to our desks, the importance of ergonomics cannot be overstated. Proper workstation setup is crucial for preventing injuries, promoting comfort, and enhancing overall job satisfaction. In this chapter, we'll explore the significance of ergonomic practices, offer practical guidelines for optimizing your office layout, and share an inspiring real-life example of a company that embraced this revolution, resulting in remarkable changes for their workforce. Get ready to discover how small adjustments can lead to monumental improvements in health and productivity!

Importance of Ergonomics

Imagine this: you arrive at work, ready to tackle the day. You sit down at your desk, but within minutes, discomfort creeps in. Your back aches, your wrists hurt, and you can't seem to concentrate. Sound familiar? This is the reality for many employees in today's fast-paced work environments.

The significance of ergonomics lies in its potential to create a workspace that supports your body's natural posture and movements. Poorly designed workstations can lead to a variety of musculoskeletal disorders, including carpal tunnel syndrome, chronic back pain, and neck strain. According to the Bureau of Labor Statistics, over 33% of workplace injuries are attributed to ergonomic issues. But here's the good news: investing in ergonomic practices not only prevents these injuries but also fosters a more engaged, productive workforce.

Ergonomic Guidelines

So, how can we revolutionize our workspaces? Here are some essential tips to optimize your office furniture and layout for maximum comfort and efficiency:

Chair Selection: Choose an adjustable chair that supports your lower back. The seat height should allow your feet to rest flat on the floor or on a footrest, with your knees at a 90-degree angle.

Look for chairs with lumbar support to promote proper spine alignment.

Desk Height: Your desk should be at elbow height when seated. A good rule of thumb is to keep your forearms parallel to the ground while typing. If your desk is too high or too low, consider using a keyboard tray or adjustable standing desk.

Monitor Positioning: Position your computer monitor about an arm's length away and at eye level to prevent neck strain. The top of the screen should be at or just below eye level. If you use multiple monitors, arrange them in a slight curve to minimize neck movement.

Keyboard and Mouse Setup: Keep your keyboard and mouse close enough to avoid overreaching. Your wrists should be straight while typing, and your elbows should remain close to your body. Consider using wrist supports to minimize strain.

Frequent Breaks: Encourage employees to take short breaks every hour to stand, stretch, and move around. This practice not only reduces physical tension but also enhances mental clarity and focus.

Real-Life Example: The Ergonomic Transformation at FlexiCorp

To illustrate the transformative power of ergonomics in the workplace, let's take a look at FlexiCorp, a company that undertook a significant office redesign focused on ergonomic principles.

The Challenge: Before the redesign, FlexiCorp faced high rates of absenteeism due to musculoskeletal injuries and complaints of discomfort among employees. Morale was low, and productivity was suffering. The leadership team recognized that the traditional office setup was not conducive to employee well-being and decided it was time for a change.

The Redesign: FlexiCorp engaged ergonomic experts to assess their office layout and provide recommendations. They invested in height-adjustable desks, ergonomic chairs with lumbar support, and improved lighting. Each workstation was tailored to the individual employee, ensuring optimal setup for comfort and productivity.

The Results: The impact of the redesign was immediate and profound. Within just six months, FlexiCorp reported a 40% decrease in injury claims and a remarkable 30% increase in overall employee satisfaction. Employees felt valued and supported, leading to a surge in morale and productivity. Team members also embraced the culture of wellness, actively participating in stretching and movement breaks throughout the day.

Sarah, a marketing executive at FlexiCorp, shared, "After the redesign, I noticed a huge difference in how I felt at work. I no longer leave the office with a sore back. I can focus better, and my productivity has soared!"

Conclusion

The Office Ergonomics Revolution is not just a trend; it's a movement toward healthier, happier work environments. By prioritizing ergonomic practices, companies can prevent injuries, boost morale, and enhance productivity.

As you reflect on your own workspace, consider the simple adjustments you can make to create a more ergonomic environment. Whether it's investing in a supportive chair, optimizing your monitor position, or encouraging regular movement breaks, every small change can lead to significant improvements in your overall well-being.

Embrace the ergonomics revolution today—your body and mind will thank you for it! Let's create workspaces that not only foster productivity but also cultivate a culture of care and well-being for everyone.

CHAPTER 16: BUILDING A SUPPORTIVE WORK CULTURE

Welcome to a transformative chapter that invites you to be a catalyst for change in your workplace! In today's fast-paced world, fostering a supportive work culture is not just a nice-to-have—it's a must-have. A thriving organizational culture not only enhances productivity but also nurtures employee well-being. In this chapter, we'll discuss how companies can promote physical well-being through proactive policies, explore ways to engage employees in wellness initiatives, and highlight a real-life example of a company that has successfully made wellness a cornerstone of its culture. Let's dive in and discover how a supportive work environment can pave the way for healthier, happier employees!

Promoting Physical Well-Being

Imagine stepping into an office where healthy living is woven into the very fabric of the work culture. Organizations that prioritize physical well-being send a powerful message: we care about you. Implementing organizational policies that encourage a healthy lifestyle can take many forms:

Flexible Work Hours: Allowing employees to adjust their work schedules can enable them to fit in exercise or attend wellness classes. Flexibility can be the difference between sitting at a desk for hours and taking a brisk walk during lunch.

Fitness Challenges: Organizing regular fitness challenges, such as step competitions or group workout sessions, can foster camaraderie while promoting physical activity. Providing incentives like prizes or recognition can motivate participation.

Wellness Days: Offering designated wellness days or half-days encourages employees to prioritize their health. Whether it's a day for self-care, outdoor activities, or simply resting, these initiatives send a clear signal that well-being is essential.

Healthy Food Options: Providing healthy snacks and meals in the workplace not only promotes good nutrition but also reinforces the importance of making better food choices. Consider partnering with local vendors to supply fresh fruits, nuts, and whole grains.

Mental Health Support: A supportive culture acknowledges

that mental and physical health are intertwined. Implementing policies that offer access to counseling services, meditation rooms, or mental health days can create a more holistic approach to well-being.

Employee Involvement

Involving employees in wellness initiatives not only enhances their effectiveness but also fosters a sense of ownership and community. Here are some engaging ways to encourage employee participation:

Wellness Committees: Establish a wellness committee comprised of employees from different departments. This committee can brainstorm, plan, and execute wellness initiatives that resonate with the workforce, ensuring everyone's voice is heard.

Feedback and Surveys: Conduct regular surveys to gather employee feedback on existing wellness programs and suggestions for new initiatives. This involvement fosters a culture of inclusivity and encourages employees to share their ideas.

Buddy Systems: Create buddy systems for wellness challenges, where employees pair up to support and motivate each other. This not only enhances accountability but also builds relationships and camaraderie.

Educational Workshops: Offer workshops on topics such as nutrition, stress management, and physical fitness. Engaging employees in their education empowers them to make informed choices about their health.

Celebrating Success: Recognize and celebrate individual and

team achievements related to wellness initiatives. Public acknowledgment reinforces positive behaviors and motivates others to participate.

Real-Life Example: HealthFirst Innovations

Let's take a closer look at HealthFirst Innovations, a technology company that has successfully implemented a comprehensive wellness program, transforming their workplace culture and enhancing employee satisfaction.

The Challenge: Before the launch of their wellness program, HealthFirst faced low employee morale, high turnover rates, and increasing healthcare costs. Leadership recognized that their employees were struggling with stress and burnout, impacting productivity and engagement.

The Program: In response, HealthFirst created a wellness program that emphasized physical health, mental well-being, and community involvement. They introduced flexible work hours, organized weekly fitness challenges, and provided access to nutrition workshops. Employees were encouraged to form wellness committees, allowing them to contribute ideas and lead initiatives.

The Results: The impact was transformative. Within a year, HealthFirst reported a staggering 25% decrease in employee turnover and a 40% increase in overall job satisfaction. Employees felt more engaged and supported, and the company's healthcare costs began to decline as health metrics improved.

Jessica, a software engineer at HealthFirst, shared, "The wellness program has completely changed my perspective on work. I now look forward to participating in fitness challenges with my colleagues. It's brought us closer together and made work so much more enjoyable!"

Conclusion

Building a supportive work culture that promotes physical well-being is not just an organizational responsibility; it's a shared journey toward a healthier and happier workplace. By implementing proactive policies and actively involving employees in wellness initiatives, companies can create an environment where well-being flourishes.

As you consider the changes you can make within your own organization, remember that even small steps can lead to significant transformations. Whether it's launching a new wellness program, gathering employee feedback, or simply creating an open dialogue about health, every action contributes to a culture that prioritizes well-being.

Let's champion a work culture where every employee feels valued, supported, and empowered to prioritize their health. Together, we can create workplaces that not only drive productivity but also nurture the physical and mental well-being of everyone involved. The time for change is now—let's get started!

CHAPTER 17: THE ROLE OF LEADERSHIP IN WELLNESS

Welcome to a pivotal chapter that underscores the significant impact of leadership on fostering a culture of health and wellness in the workplace! Leadership isn't just about making decisions; it's about setting the tone for a thriving environment where employees feel valued, motivated, and encouraged to prioritize their well-being. In this chapter, we'll explore how effective leaders influence wellness culture, share strategies for fostering engagement, and highlight a real-life example of an organization that has redefined leadership through wellness initiatives. Let's embark on this journey of inspiring leadership that champions well-being!

Leadership's Influence

Imagine walking into a workplace where the air is infused with positivity and energy—where employees are not only productive but genuinely happy. This environment doesn't happen by chance; it is cultivated by strong leadership. Leaders play a crucial role in establishing a culture of health and wellness, and their influence can be felt at every level of the organization.

Setting the Vision: Leaders must articulate a clear vision of well-being that resonates throughout the organization. By prioritizing health and wellness, leaders signal to employees that their well-being is a core value. This vision can include goals such as promoting work-life balance, encouraging physical activity, and fostering mental health support.

Leading by Example: Actions speak louder than words. When leaders model healthy behaviors—whether it's taking breaks to exercise, participating in wellness challenges, or openly discussing mental health—they set a powerful example for employees. This visible commitment can inspire others to adopt similar practices.

Open Communication: A culture of health thrives on open communication. Leaders should encourage conversations about well-being, actively listen to employee feedback, and create channels for sharing ideas and concerns. Transparency fosters trust and empowers employees to take ownership of their health.

Creating a Supportive Environment: Leaders are responsible for creating an environment where employees feel safe to prioritize their wellness. This includes providing resources, flexible work arrangements, and programs that support mental and physical health.

Recognizing Achievements: Celebrating employee successes related to health and wellness reinforces the importance of these initiatives. Acknowledgment can come in many forms—awards, shout-outs in meetings, or wellness milestones shared company-wide.

Fostering Engagement

Engagement is the key to a successful wellness culture, and leaders play a vital role in fostering this engagement. Here are some strategies to effectively promote and model healthy behaviors within the organization:

Wellness Ambassadors: Encourage employees to become wellness ambassadors. This program empowers selected individuals to promote health initiatives, organize activities, and serve as champions of wellness within their teams. By involving employees in leadership roles, organizations create a sense of community and shared responsibility.

Wellness Workshops: Host regular workshops that focus on various aspects of wellness, from nutrition and fitness to mental health and stress management. Leaders should participate in these workshops, demonstrating their commitment to personal growth and wellness education.

Feedback Mechanisms: Create feedback mechanisms that allow

employees to share their thoughts on wellness initiatives. Surveys, suggestion boxes, and open forums provide valuable insights and make employees feel involved in the decision-making process.

Incentives and Challenges: Leaders can initiate friendly competitions and wellness challenges, providing incentives for participation. Whether it's a step challenge or a nutrition month, these initiatives can spark enthusiasm and motivate employees to engage in healthier habits.

Work-Life Balance Policies: Implement policies that support work-life balance, such as flexible work hours, remote work options, and mandatory time off. By prioritizing these practices, leaders demonstrate that employee well-being is non-negotiable.

Real-Life Example: ThriveWell Solutions

Let's take a closer look at ThriveWell Solutions, a healthcare technology company that has effectively integrated wellness into its leadership practices, fostering an engaged and healthy workforce.

The Challenge: Prior to implementing their wellness initiatives, ThriveWell experienced high employee turnover and declining morale. Leadership recognized that they needed to revamp their approach to create a more supportive and health-focused environment.

The Program: ThriveWell's leadership team embarked on a journey to redefine their workplace culture. They established a vision that prioritized wellness at all levels of the organization. Leaders began participating in fitness classes, hosting wellness workshops, and openly discussing mental health challenges in team meetings. They also created a wellness committee comprising employees from various departments to drive engagement and collect feedback.

The Results: The transformation was remarkable. Within two years, ThriveWell reported a 30% decrease in turnover and a 50% increase in employee engagement scores. Employees felt empowered to prioritize their health, and morale soared.

David, the CEO of ThriveWell, shared, "When we made wellness a priority, everything changed. Our employees felt supported, engaged, and motivated. It's amazing what happens when leadership takes the initiative to champion health and well-being!"

Conclusion

The role of leadership in promoting wellness is paramount. Leaders have the power to set the tone for a culture that values health, fosters engagement, and inspires employees to prioritize their well-being. By leading by example, encouraging open communication, and implementing supportive policies, leaders can create an environment where wellness thrives.

As you consider your own leadership journey, remember that every action counts. Whether it's actively participating in wellness initiatives, supporting employee feedback, or setting clear wellness goals, your commitment can spark a positive shift in your organization.

Let's champion leadership that prioritizes well-being, creates healthier workplaces, and empowers employees to thrive both personally and professionally. Together, we can foster a culture of health that transforms not just organizations, but lives. The future of work is well, and it starts with you!

CHAPTER 18: WELLNESS CHALLENGES: FUN AND ENGAGING ACTIVITIES

Welcome to the exciting world of workplace wellness challenges! In this chapter, we'll explore how to make health and well-being a lively, engaging, and community-building experience in your organization. Wellness challenges not only inspire employees to adopt healthier habits but also foster camaraderie and a sense of belonging. Whether it's a step challenge, a healthy eating contest, or mindfulness practices, these activities can invigorate your workplace culture and boost morale. Let's dive into some engaging ideas, metrics to measure success, and a real-life example that showcases the transformative power of wellness challenges!

Engaging Activities

Creating engaging wellness challenges doesn't have to be complicated. In fact, the best activities are often simple, fun, and inclusive. Here are some ideas to spark participation and camaraderie among your team:

Step Challenge: Organize a company-wide step challenge using fitness trackers or mobile apps. Encourage teams to set collective goals, compete for prizes, and share their progress. A little friendly competition can motivate employees to move more!

Healthy Eating Contest: Host a healthy recipe contest where employees can showcase their culinary skills. Participants can bring in their dishes for a potluck-style tasting. Offer prizes for the most creative, healthiest, and tastiest recipes. This not only promotes healthier eating but also fosters community through shared meals.

Mindfulness Challenge: Introduce a mindfulness challenge that encourages employees to practice mindfulness exercises daily. This could include meditation, deep-breathing exercises, or gratitude journaling. Create a group where participants can share their experiences and tips, fostering a supportive environment.

Fitness Bingo: Create a bingo card filled with different wellness activities such as "take a 10-minute walk," "drink eight glasses of water," or "try a new workout class." Employees can work towards completing their bingo card over a month, and those who complete a row can earn prizes.

Team Sports Day: Organize a fun day of team sports like soccer, volleyball, or relay races. This not only gets everyone moving but also encourages teamwork and strengthens relationships among colleagues.

Weekly Wellness Workshops: Offer weekly workshops focused on various health topics, such as nutrition, stress management, or exercise. Invite experts or encourage team members to share their knowledge. Engaging in learning together promotes a culture of health and wellness.

Charity Walk/Run: Participate as a team in a local charity walk or run. Not only does this promote fitness, but it also supports a good cause. The shared experience of training and participating can strengthen team bonds.

Measuring Success

To ensure that your wellness challenges are effective, it's important to measure their success. Here are some metrics to consider when evaluating your activities:

Participation Rates: Track the number of employees participating in each challenge. A high participation rate indicates strong interest and engagement in wellness initiatives.

Behavior Change: Monitor changes in employee habits, such as increased physical activity, healthier eating choices, or improved stress management. Surveys or self-reported data can help measure these changes.

Employee Feedback: Conduct surveys to gather feedback from participants about their experiences. Ask what they enjoyed, what they found challenging, and how they believe the activities impacted their well-being.

Team Dynamics: Assess improvements in teamwork and collaboration. You can evaluate this through team surveys or observations of interactions during challenges.

Health Metrics: If feasible, measure changes in health metrics such as weight, cholesterol levels, or overall fitness. Encouraging employees to share these results (voluntarily) can inspire others to join future challenges.

Employee Morale: Evaluate overall employee morale and job satisfaction before and after the challenges. Positive changes in morale can indicate the effectiveness of wellness initiatives in creating a supportive work environment.

Real-Life Example: The Fit for Fun Challenge

Let's take a look at Tech Innovations Inc., a mid-sized tech company that implemented a Fit for Fun Challenge to promote wellness and boost team morale.

The Challenge: Tech Innovations decided to launch a month-long step challenge to encourage employees to become more active while fostering a sense of community. Teams were formed, and each was tasked with reaching a combined goal of 10,000 steps per week.

The Execution: Employees were encouraged to share their progress via a dedicated chat group. Each week featured mini-competitions, such as who could take the most steps in a day or the most creative way to incorporate movement into their routines (like walking meetings or dancing breaks). They offered weekly prizes for the highest steppers, and participation was high!

The Results: By the end of the month, over 70% of employees had participated, and the company recorded an impressive increase in overall physical activity levels. Employee surveys revealed that 90% felt more connected to their colleagues, and 85% reported feeling more energized at work.

Testimonials

Here are a few testimonials from participants that highlight the success of the Fit for Fun Challenge:

Anna, Software Developer: "I never thought I'd enjoy walking so much! The challenge pushed me to get outside and explore the city during my breaks. Plus, I loved bonding with my team!"

Mark, Project Manager: "The competition made me more accountable for my activity. I've not only lost a few pounds, but I've also made new friends at work. It feels great to be part of a team that values health!"

Sophia, HR Manager: "The step challenge was a game-changer! It transformed the atmosphere in our office. We all cheered each other on, and it was amazing to see so many people excited about moving more."

Conclusion

Wellness challenges can ignite a spark of enthusiasm and camaraderie in any workplace. By implementing engaging activities, measuring success, and showcasing real-life examples, you can create a culture where health and well-being are not only prioritized but celebrated.

As leaders and team members, it's our responsibility to foster environments that encourage participation in wellness initiatives. Remember, health doesn't have to be a chore; it can be fun, engaging, and deeply rewarding. Embrace these challenges as a way to promote a vibrant and connected workplace, and watch as your organization flourishes with renewed energy and morale. Let's make wellness a movement, and together, we can achieve great things!

CHAPTER 19: USING TECHNOLOGY TO PROMOTE HEALTH

Welcome to the future of wellness! In today's fast-paced world, technology has become an invaluable ally in our quest for health and well-being. With the right tools and apps at our fingertips, we can transform our approach to fitness, nutrition, mental wellness, and overall health. In this chapter, we'll explore the digital resources available to support health and wellness in the workplace, discover how gamification can make wellness fun and engaging, and hear firsthand accounts from employees who have successfully integrated technology into their daily health habits. Let's embark on this exciting journey to harness technology for a healthier, happier workforce!

Health Apps and Tools

Digital resources are revolutionizing how we manage our health. Health apps and tools can track progress, provide personalized recommendations, and foster connections within the workplace community. Here are some categories of health apps that can support your well-being journey:

Fitness Trackers: Wearable devices like Fitbit, Apple Watch, and Garmin track physical activity, heart rate, and sleep patterns. These trackers motivate users to meet their fitness goals and monitor their progress. Many devices also sync with smartphone apps, allowing for more detailed insights into overall health.

Nutrition Apps: Apps such as MyFitnessPal and Lose It! help users track their food intake and analyze nutritional value. They can set personalized goals for caloric intake and macronutrients, making healthy eating easier. Many of these apps also feature barcode scanners for quick food logging.

Mindfulness and Meditation Apps: Headspace, Calm, and Insight Timer offer guided meditations, sleep stories, and mindfulness exercises. These apps help employees manage stress and enhance focus, making them perfect for integrating mindfulness practices into daily routines.

Exercise and Workout Apps: From workout planning to guided

exercise sessions, apps like Nike Training Club, Fitbit Coach, and Peloton offer a range of routines for every fitness level. These platforms often provide access to on-demand classes, making it easy to fit a workout into a busy schedule.

Health and Wellness Communities: Platforms like Strava or Fitocracy encourage users to connect with others, share accomplishments, and participate in challenges. These communities foster a sense of accountability and motivation among peers.

Gamification of Wellness

Gone are the days when wellness was viewed as a chore. With gamification, we can turn health and fitness into an engaging, enjoyable experience. Gamification involves incorporating game-like elements into non-game contexts, and it can be particularly effective in promoting workplace wellness. Here's how technology can gamify health initiatives:

Challenge Competitions: Implement friendly competitions among employees, such as step contests, hydration challenges, or fitness goals. Apps can facilitate these competitions, allowing participants to track progress, earn points, and climb leaderboards.

Rewards Systems: Many wellness apps feature rewards systems where users earn points for completing tasks. These points can be redeemed for real-world rewards, such as gift cards, extra vacation days, or wellness-related prizes. This incentivizes participation and commitment to health goals.

Personalized Avatars and Progress Tracking: Users can create avatars and track their progress visually within wellness apps. This can add an element of fun and personalization, encouraging users to engage consistently and celebrate their achievements.

Social Sharing: Encourage employees to share their progress and achievements on social media platforms or internal communication tools. This not only fosters community support but also creates a culture of celebration around health and wellness.

Daily Challenges and Mini-Games: Incorporate daily challenges or mini-games into wellness programs. These could be as simple as logging a healthy meal or completing a five-minute mindfulness exercise. The short, manageable nature of these tasks makes them easier to fit into busy schedules, and employees are more likely to participate.

Real-Life Example: Employee Favorites in Wellness Tech

Let's take a moment to hear from employees at Innovate Tech, a dynamic software company committed to promoting health and well-being. They've embraced technology as a cornerstone of their wellness initiatives, and employees have shared their favorite wellness apps, highlighting the positive impact on their daily habits.

David, Software Engineer: "I love using MyFitnessPal! It makes tracking my meals so easy, and I've learned so much about nutrition. I've lost 15 pounds and feel more energetic at work. Plus, the barcode scanner makes logging super quick!"

Sara, Marketing Manager: "Headspace has been a game-changer for me. I use it every morning for meditation, and it sets a positive tone for my day. I feel less stressed and more focused during meetings. It's an essential part of my routine now!"

Jake, UX Designer: "I'm a huge fan of Fitbit. It's not just about steps for me; it tracks my sleep patterns too! Understanding my sleep quality has motivated me to prioritize getting to bed earlier. I've noticed a real difference in my productivity."

Emily, HR Specialist: "Strava has transformed my running routine! I love the community aspect. Seeing my colleagues' achievements keeps me motivated, and the friendly competition pushes me to improve my times."

Tom, Project Manager: "The Peloton app is my go-to for workouts. I can choose classes that fit my schedule, whether it's a quick 20-minute ride or a longer strength training session. Plus, the live classes with friends add a fun twist!"

Conclusion

As we've seen, technology offers a wealth of resources to support health and wellness in the workplace. By leveraging health apps, gamifying wellness initiatives, and fostering community engagement, organizations can create an environment that prioritizes employee well-being.

Embrace the digital revolution in health and wellness, and encourage employees to explore the tools that resonate with them. Remember, wellness doesn't have to be a solitary journey; it can be a shared adventure, filled with excitement, encouragement, and celebration. Together, let's harness the power of technology to build a healthier, happier workplace— one app, one challenge, and one employee at a time!

CHAPTER 20: OVERCOMIN G BARRIERS TO HEALTHY LIVING

In our pursuit of a healthier lifestyle, we often encounter barriers that can seem insurmountable. From demanding work schedules to limited access to resources, the challenges can feel overwhelming. But fear not! This chapter is here to inspire you to face these obstacles head-on with actionable strategies and real-life success stories that prove a healthier lifestyle is within your reach. Together, we'll identify common challenges and develop practical solutions that will empower you to prioritize your well-being, no matter how busy life gets.

Common Obstacles

Let's start by identifying some of the most common barriers employees face in maintaining physical well-being:

Time Constraints: Between work deadlines, family commitments, and social obligations, finding time to focus on health can feel impossible. Busy professionals often struggle to carve out moments for exercise, meal prep, or relaxation.

Lack of Resources: Not everyone has access to fitness facilities, healthy food options, or wellness programs. Some employees work in environments where such resources are limited, making it harder to prioritize health.

Motivation and Energy: After long hours at work, the thought of hitting the gym or preparing a nutritious meal can feel daunting. Fatigue can sap motivation, leading to unhealthy habits that spiral out of control.

Workplace Culture: A lack of support from colleagues or a workplace that prioritizes long hours over well-being can hinder individual efforts to lead a healthier lifestyle. If the culture doesn't value health, employees may feel discouraged from making changes.

Knowledge Gaps: Many people aren't aware of how to make healthier choices or how to integrate wellness practices into their lives. Misinformation about nutrition and exercise can also create confusion.

Problem-Solving Strategies

Now that we've identified these barriers, let's explore some actionable solutions to overcome them:

Time Management Techniques: Start by prioritizing health in your schedule. Consider blocking out specific times for exercise, meal prep, or relaxation, just as you would for any important meeting. Use productivity techniques like the Pomodoro method to stay focused and include short exercise breaks during work sessions. Even 10 minutes of movement can make a difference!

Leverage Technology: Use fitness apps to plan quick workouts and track progress. Online resources, including cooking videos and nutrition blogs, can help you find healthy recipes that are easy to prepare. Virtual workout classes provide flexibility to exercise at home or during breaks.

Start Small: Focus on incremental changes rather than an all-or-nothing approach. Incorporate more fruits and vegetables into your meals, take the stairs instead of the elevator, or commit to a 5-minute stretching routine. These small victories can build momentum and motivate you to take on bigger challenges.

Create a Supportive Environment: Seek out colleagues or friends who share your health goals. Forming a buddy system or accountability group can provide the encouragement and motivation needed to stay committed. Share healthy recipes, organize group workouts, or plan wellness challenges together to foster a culture of health.

Advocate for Workplace Wellness: Encourage your employer to invest in wellness programs that provide resources and support for healthy living. This could include offering gym memberships, healthy snacks in the breakroom, or wellness workshops. A collective voice can lead to meaningful changes that benefit everyone.

Educate Yourself: Take the initiative to learn more about nutrition, exercise, and wellness practices. Attend workshops, read books, or follow credible sources online. The more informed you are, the easier it will be to make healthier choices.

Real-Life Example: A Team's Transformation

Let's take a look at The Green Team, a dedicated group of employees at Eco Solutions, a company focused on sustainability. Despite their commitment to environmental health, many team members struggled to maintain their physical well-being. Recognizing the challenges they faced, they decided to take action.

Identifying the Challenge: Time constraints and a lack of resources were the primary barriers. Employees often worked long hours and felt too exhausted to exercise. The cafeteria offered limited healthy options, making it difficult to eat well during the day.

Creating a Plan: The team held a brainstorming session to identify solutions. They committed to implementing short, structured wellness breaks throughout the day, where employees could engage in quick workouts, stretches, or mindfulness exercises. They also collaborated with management to improve cafeteria offerings, introducing healthier snacks and meals.

Building a Community: The Green Team started a weekly wellness challenge, encouraging everyone to track their steps, try new healthy recipes, and support one another. They created a group chat to share tips, motivation, and progress. Employees also organized lunch-and-learn sessions, where they invited local health professionals to discuss nutrition and wellness.

Seeing Results: Within a few months, the team experienced significant improvements. Employee engagement soared, as did productivity. The camaraderie built through shared goals fostered a positive work culture, and many employees reported feeling more energized and focused. The cafeteria's new menu was met with enthusiasm, with healthier options becoming popular among the staff.

Transformative Impact: Perhaps the most inspiring outcome was the team's collective mindset shift. What began as individual struggles transformed into a culture of wellness. Employees became advocates for their health, inspiring others within the organization to take charge of their well-being.

Conclusion

Overcoming barriers to healthy living is not just about individual effort; it's about community, collaboration, and commitment. By identifying challenges and implementing practical solutions, you can take meaningful steps toward a healthier lifestyle. Remember that every small change adds up, and with the right mindset and support, you can achieve your health and wellness goals.

Embrace the journey, stay motivated, and remind yourself that obstacles are merely stepping stones toward success. Together, let's create a culture of health and wellness in the workplace that empowers every employee to thrive—because when you prioritize well-being, you not only enhance your own life but also inspire those around you. Your path to better health starts today!

CHAPTER 21: ENGAGING EMPLOYEES IN THEIR HEALTH JOURNEY

In today's fast-paced work environment, engaging employees in their health and wellness journey is not just beneficial—it's essential. When employees are actively involved in their own health, organizations see increased productivity, reduced absenteeism, and enhanced morale. This chapter will explore innovative strategies to foster an inclusive environment where employees feel motivated to participate in wellness programs. We'll discuss the significance of feedback mechanisms and showcase a real-life example of a company that has successfully engaged its workforce in health initiatives through creative programming and effective communication.

Participation Strategies

Engaging employees in their health journey requires thoughtful strategies that resonate with their needs and interests. Here are several proven methods to foster participation:

Create a Culture of Health: Start by integrating wellness into the company culture. Make health a shared value by showcasing success stories, celebrating milestones, and regularly communicating the importance of well-being. When employees see health as a priority for the organization, they are more likely to engage.

Offer Diverse Wellness Programs: Recognize that employees have varied interests and needs. Implement a range of wellness programs that cater to different lifestyles—think fitness challenges, mental health workshops, nutrition seminars, and mindfulness sessions. Providing options ensures that everyone can find something that resonates with them.

Make Wellness Fun: Incorporate gamification into wellness programs to make participation exciting. Create friendly competitions, offer incentives for achieving health goals, and organize themed events such as "Wellness Wednesdays" or "Fit Fridays." When health initiatives are enjoyable, employees are more likely to join in.

Involve Employees in Program Development: Give employees a

voice in shaping wellness initiatives. Form wellness committees that include representatives from different departments and levels of the organization. This inclusivity ensures that programs meet the unique needs of the workforce and fosters a sense of ownership.

Promote Social Connections: Encourage team-based activities that build camaraderie and promote healthy living. Organize group fitness classes, walking clubs, or wellness retreats that enable employees to bond while prioritizing their health. The social aspect can significantly boost participation rates.

Leverage Technology: Use health apps and online platforms to enhance engagement. Consider implementing wellness challenges through apps that allow employees to track their progress, share achievements, and interact with colleagues. The convenience of technology can motivate participation and foster community.

Feedback Mechanisms

Gathering employee input is crucial for enhancing wellness programs and ensuring they remain relevant and effective. Here's how to create effective feedback mechanisms:

Conduct Surveys and Polls: Regularly distribute surveys to assess employee interests, preferences, and experiences with wellness programs. Use anonymous feedback to encourage honest responses, which can provide valuable insights into what works and what needs improvement.

Host Focus Groups: Organize small group discussions where employees can voice their opinions and suggest ideas for wellness initiatives. Focus groups foster open dialogue and allow for in-depth exploration of employee needs, which can lead to more tailored programming.

Create Suggestion Boxes: Provide physical or digital suggestion boxes where employees can submit ideas or feedback at any time. This simple yet effective method empowers employees to share their thoughts without the pressure of a formal setting.

Regularly Review and Adapt Programs: Make it a practice to evaluate wellness programs periodically based on the feedback received. Be transparent about how employee input shapes programming decisions, and communicate any changes made as a result. This shows employees that their voices matter.

Celebrate Progress and Success: Share the results of wellness initiatives with the entire organization. Highlight how employee feedback has led to improvements, and recognize individual or team successes. Celebrating achievements reinforces the value of participation and motivates continued engagement.

Real-Life Example: HealthFirst Innovations

Let's look at HealthFirst Innovations, a tech company that has mastered the art of engaging employees in their health journey. Recognizing that employee well-being directly impacts productivity and job satisfaction, they embarked on a mission to create a culture of health that resonates throughout the organization.

Engaging Participation: HealthFirst began by conducting an extensive survey to understand employees' wellness interests and needs. They learned that their workforce was diverse, with varying preferences for fitness activities and wellness programs. As a response, they launched a multifaceted wellness initiative that included options like yoga classes, mental health workshops, nutrition challenges, and team sports leagues.

Incentivizing Fun: To foster enthusiasm, they gamified their wellness programs through friendly competitions. Employees could earn points for participating in activities, attending workshops, and reaching personal health milestones. These points translated into rewards, from gift cards to extra vacation days. This approach not only motivated employees but also cultivated a sense of camaraderie as teams rallied together to achieve common goals.

Feedback as a Foundation: HealthFirst established a wellness committee made up of employees from various departments, ensuring that all voices were heard. They regularly conducted feedback surveys and hosted focus groups to gather insights on the effectiveness of their programs. Employees felt empowered, knowing that their input directly influenced the development and improvement of wellness initiatives.

Communicating Success: The company made it a point to celebrate successes—big and small. They featured employee testimonials in company newsletters, highlighting personal health journeys and the positive impact of the wellness programs. By showcasing these stories, HealthFirst not only motivated others to participate but also reinforced the notion that the company genuinely cared about its employees' well-being.

Measurable Impact: Over the course of a year, HealthFirst saw remarkable improvements. Participation in wellness programs soared by 75%, and employees reported higher job satisfaction and lower stress levels. The culture of health became ingrained in the organization, creating a ripple effect that benefited everyone.

Conclusion

Engaging employees in their health journey is a shared responsibility that can transform workplace culture. By fostering an inclusive environment, implementing diverse wellness programs, and establishing feedback mechanisms, organizations can empower their workforce to take charge of their health. The success story of HealthFirst Innovations serves as a testament to the incredible potential that lies in prioritizing employee well-being.

Let this chapter inspire you to take action—whether you're a leader looking to enhance your organization's wellness initiatives or an employee eager to advocate for your health. Together, we can create a vibrant, health-focused workplace where everyone thrives. Remember, the journey to better health begins with engagement, and your involvement can lead to positive change for you and your organization!

CHAPTER 22: CELEBRATIN G SUCCESS: RECOGNIZIN G WELLNESS ACHIEVEME NTS

Celebrating success is an integral part of any wellness

program, but it goes beyond just acknowledging achievements; it serves as a powerful motivator that can ignite enthusiasm and engagement within an organization. When employees feel recognized for their efforts in maintaining their health and well-being, it fosters a sense of community and belonging, leading to increased morale and continued participation. In this chapter, we will explore the importance of recognition in wellness initiatives, provide inspiring celebration ideas, and share real-life examples of employee recognition stories that highlight how celebrations can create a positive work culture.

Importance of Recognition

Recognition is a fundamental human need. When individuals see their efforts acknowledged, it enhances their motivation, reinforces positive behavior, and encourages them to continue striving for their goals. Here are several compelling reasons why celebrating wellness achievements is crucial:

Boosts Morale: Acknowledging employees' hard work and dedication fosters a sense of accomplishment. This uplifted morale not only makes employees feel valued but also enhances their overall job satisfaction, leading to a happier workplace.

Encourages Continued Participation: When employees see that their efforts are recognized, they are more likely to engage in wellness initiatives consistently. Celebration acts as a powerful incentive, motivating individuals to stay committed to their health journeys.

Strengthens Community: Recognition celebrations create opportunities for connection and camaraderie among employees. Celebrating milestones together fosters teamwork and cultivates a sense of belonging, making employees feel more invested in the organization.

Reinforces Organizational Values: A culture of recognition aligns with the values of well-being and health that organizations strive to promote. Celebrating wellness achievements signals that the company genuinely cares about its employees' health, further embedding these values into the workplace culture.

Celebration Ideas

Organizations can implement various creative recognition methods to celebrate wellness achievements effectively. Here are some ideas that can make celebrations memorable:

Wellness Awards: Host a quarterly or annual awards ceremony recognizing individuals or teams that have made significant strides in their health journeys. Categories could include "Most Improved," "Best Team Player," or "Wellness Champion." Awards can include trophies, certificates, or gift cards, adding an element of excitement.

Feature Stories: Highlight employee wellness journeys in company newsletters, on bulletin boards, or through social media channels. Sharing personal stories of transformation and success not only recognizes individuals but also inspires others to embark on their wellness paths.

Wellness Celebrations: Organize wellness-themed events, such as health fairs, wellness week, or "Fit Fridays," where employees can participate in activities like group workouts, cooking demos, or mindfulness sessions. Celebrating achievements during these events can create a festive atmosphere.

Peer Recognition Programs: Implement a peer-to-peer recognition program where employees can nominate colleagues for their health efforts. This not only fosters appreciation among employees but also promotes a culture of support and encouragement.

Health Milestone Commemorations: Celebrate personal milestones, such as weight loss achievements, completion of fitness challenges, or reaching a long-term health goal. Acknowledging these individual journeys during team meetings or company-wide gatherings can boost motivation.

Wellness Raffles: Hold raffles for those who have participated in wellness programs or achieved specific goals. Prizes can range from fitness gear to wellness retreats, creating excitement and encouraging ongoing participation.

Real-Life Example: The Journey at WellnessWorks

WellnessWorks, a mid-sized company, recognized the power of celebrating wellness achievements and integrated this principle into their workplace culture. From the outset, their leadership understood that fostering a supportive environment was crucial for employee engagement in wellness initiatives.

Creating Meaningful Recognition: To cultivate a culture of recognition, WellnessWorks introduced their annual "Wellness Awards Night," where employees were celebrated for their health achievements over the year. The event included a dinner, awards presentation, and motivational talks from employees who had transformed their lives through wellness programs. This created a buzz of anticipation and excitement leading up to the event.

Employee Spotlights: Throughout the year, WellnessWorks featured employee wellness stories in their internal newsletter, showcasing the journeys of those who had made significant progress. Employees shared their challenges and triumphs, creating a ripple effect of inspiration across the organization. These stories resonated deeply, motivating others to join in and pursue their health goals.

Celebrating Milestones: When one employee, Sarah, achieved a remarkable 50-pound weight loss through the company's wellness program, her success was celebrated widely. Sarah was not only awarded "Most Improved" but also had her story shared during the Wellness Awards Night, inspiring many colleagues to engage in their health journeys. The overwhelming support from her peers made her feel valued and motivated to maintain her progress.

Impact on Culture: As a result of these celebrations, WellnessWorks saw an impressive 60% increase in employee participation in wellness initiatives over two years. Employees reported higher job satisfaction and a sense of community, with many stating that they felt more connected to their colleagues.

Conclusion

Celebrating success is an essential ingredient in the recipe for a thriving workplace wellness culture. By recognizing employee achievements, organizations can boost morale, encourage continued participation, and create a sense of community. The ideas presented in this chapter are not just suggestions; they are opportunities to foster a positive work environment where wellness is celebrated and valued.

Let the example of WellnessWorks inspire you to embrace recognition as a vital part of your organization's wellness initiatives. Remember, every small victory deserves acknowledgment. When you celebrate milestones, you not only uplift individuals but also foster an environment where health and well-being thrive. Together, let's create a culture of celebration that empowers every employee to take charge of their health journey, ensuring that wellness is not just a goal, but a cherished part of everyday life!

CHAPTER 23: THE LONG-TERM BENEFITS OF INVESTING IN HEALTH

In today's fast-paced work environment, organizations often grapple with the question: Is investing in employee health worth it? The answer is a resounding yes! Investing in health and wellness initiatives is not merely a trend; it's a long-term strategy that yields impressive returns on investment (ROI) in terms of productivity, employee satisfaction, and overall organizational success. In this chapter, we will explore the financial and productivity returns of investing in employee wellness, delve into longitudinal studies showcasing sustained benefits over time, and present a real-life example of a successful wellness program that illustrates the remarkable cost savings and productivity increases achievable through strategic health investments.

ROI of Wellness Initiatives

The financial implications of investing in employee wellness are profound. When organizations allocate resources to promote health and well-being, they reap substantial rewards that far exceed their initial investments. Here are key points to consider:

Reduced Healthcare Costs: Healthier employees mean lower healthcare expenses. Research indicates that companies can save an average of $3.27 for every dollar spent on wellness programs due to decreased medical claims and reduced hospital visits.

Increased Productivity: Wellness programs lead to enhanced employee performance. According to studies, companies that invest in wellness see productivity boosts of 10% to 20%. Employees who are physically and mentally fit are more focused, engaged, and capable of producing high-quality work.

Lower Absenteeism: Employee wellness directly correlates with reduced absenteeism. Healthier employees take fewer sick days, which translates to a more consistent workforce and a significant decrease in costs associated with temporary replacements.

Enhanced Employee Retention: Organizations that prioritize

wellness are more likely to retain top talent. Investing in employee health shows that a company values its employees, fostering loyalty and reducing turnover. The cost of replacing an employee can range from 50% to 200% of their annual salary; thus, retaining staff through wellness initiatives proves financially beneficial.

Improved Employee Engagement: A culture of wellness fosters a sense of community and belonging, leading to higher levels of employee engagement. Engaged employees are not only more productive but also more likely to contribute positively to the company culture.

Longitudinal Studies

Numerous longitudinal studies underscore the sustained benefits of wellness programs over time, illustrating their enduring impact on employee health and productivity. Here are some significant findings:

Harvard University Study: A long-term study conducted by Harvard University tracked the health outcomes of employees participating in wellness programs over several years. Results showed that employees who engaged in wellness initiatives experienced significant improvements in physical health, including reduced cholesterol levels and lower blood pressure. These health benefits persisted even after the program's conclusion, emphasizing the long-term value of investing in employee wellness.

Worksite Health Promotion Programs: The American Journal of Health Promotion published a study analyzing worksite health promotion programs over a five-year period. The findings revealed that organizations with comprehensive wellness initiatives experienced sustained reductions in healthcare costs and a consistent increase in productivity. The study concluded that effective wellness programs create lasting changes in employee behavior, resulting in ongoing benefits for both individuals and organizations.

Meta-Analysis Findings: A meta-analysis of multiple studies on workplace wellness programs highlighted that the positive effects of health initiatives were not just immediate but extended for years after the programs were implemented. Participants demonstrated healthier lifestyles, greater job satisfaction, and a consistent commitment to their well-being long after their initial engagement with wellness initiatives.

Real-Life Example: The Success of HealthFirst Corp.

HealthFirst Corp., a mid-sized technology company, recognized the potential of investing in employee health. Faced with high healthcare costs and decreasing employee morale, the leadership decided to implement a comprehensive wellness program aimed at enhancing employee well-being.

The Wellness Program: HealthFirst introduced a multifaceted wellness initiative, including fitness challenges, nutrition workshops, mental health resources, and access to onsite fitness facilities. They also encouraged employees to take part in monthly health screenings and provided incentives for participating in wellness activities.

Financial Analysis: After three years of implementing the wellness program, HealthFirst conducted a thorough financial analysis to measure the program's effectiveness:

Healthcare Cost Savings: The company noted a 25% reduction in healthcare costs, translating to $500,000 in savings over three years. Employees' participation in preventive care led to fewer chronic health issues, significantly decreasing medical expenses.

Productivity Increases: Productivity metrics revealed a remarkable 15% increase in overall employee output. Employees reported feeling more energized and motivated due to the supportive wellness culture.

Employee Retention: Turnover rates dropped by 40%, saving the company an estimated $300,000 in recruitment and training costs for new hires.

Overall ROI: In total, HealthFirst Corp. realized a $3.50 return for every dollar spent on wellness initiatives, underscoring the financial advantages of investing in employee health.

Employee Feedback: Beyond the financial gains, employee satisfaction surveys reflected a significant boost in morale. Employees felt more valued and appreciated, creating a positive work environment where they were motivated to perform at their best. Testimonials from staff highlighted how the wellness program had positively impacted their lives, both personally and professionally.

Conclusion

Investing in employee health is a strategic decision that offers profound long-term benefits. The ROI of wellness initiatives extends beyond financial gains; it enhances productivity, reduces absenteeism, improves retention, and fosters a thriving workplace culture. Longitudinal studies consistently demonstrate that the positive effects of wellness programs endure over time, affirming that investing in health is not a fleeting trend but a sustainable approach to organizational success.

Let the success story of HealthFirst Corp. inspire your organization to embrace the long-term benefits of wellness initiatives. By investing in the health of your employees, you are not just improving their lives; you are laying the foundation for a thriving, productive, and engaged workforce. Together, let's champion a culture of health that benefits individuals and organizations alike—because a healthy workplace is a successful workplace!

CHAPTER 24: STAYING ACTIVE BEYOND THE OFFICE

In the fast-paced world of work, it's all too easy to become tethered to our desks, our screens, and our busy schedules. Yet, the secret to sustained productivity, creativity, and overall well-being lies not just within the walls of our workplaces but in the vibrant activities that await us beyond them. Staying active outside of work hours is not merely a luxury; it's a necessity. This chapter will explore the importance of encouraging physical activity after work, the power of community engagement through team initiatives, and inspiring real-life examples that illustrate how after-work activities foster camaraderie, joy, and lasting connections.

The Importance of Staying Active Outside of Work Hours

Why is staying active beyond the office so crucial? The benefits extend far beyond just physical health. Here are some key points to consider:

Mental Refreshment: Engaging in physical activity after a long day at work can work wonders for our mental health. Exercise releases endorphins, the body's natural mood lifters. Whether it's a brisk walk, a dance class, or a group sports game, moving your body helps clear your mind, reduce stress, and recharge your focus for the next day.

Work-Life Balance: Striking a healthy work-life balance is essential for long-term job satisfaction and personal happiness. Incorporating physical activity into your routine helps create boundaries between work and personal life, allowing you to disconnect from work demands and connect with your passions.

Strengthened Social Bonds: Participating in after-work activities provides an opportunity to strengthen relationships with colleagues in a relaxed, informal environment. Shared experiences foster trust and camaraderie, which can translate to better teamwork and collaboration back at the office.

Boosted Creativity: Stepping away from work and engaging in creative physical activities can enhance problem-solving skills and innovation. A change of scenery and routine stimulates our minds, allowing us to approach challenges from fresh perspectives.

Long-Term Health Benefits: Regular physical activity reduces the risk of chronic diseases, enhances cardiovascular health, and contributes to a longer, healthier life. Prioritizing movement outside of work contributes to a holistic approach to wellness that encompasses both physical and mental well-being.

Community Engagement: Team Activities and Initiatives

Organizations that encourage community engagement through team activities foster a culture of health and wellness while building strong connections among employees. Here are some engaging initiatives to consider:

Sports Leagues: Forming company sports teams—whether it's soccer, basketball, or volleyball—encourages friendly competition and teamwork. Participating in leagues not only promotes physical fitness but also cultivates a sense of belonging and camaraderie among team members.

Group Fitness Classes: Offering group fitness classes such as yoga, Zumba, or cycling can motivate employees to stay active together. Classes create a shared goal and sense of accountability, making exercise more enjoyable and less daunting.

Outdoor Adventure Clubs: Establishing clubs that focus on outdoor activities—like hiking, biking, or kayaking—can inspire employees to explore new passions. These clubs offer opportunities for team bonding while encouraging a healthy lifestyle.

Wellness Challenges: Organizing friendly competitions, like step challenges or fitness challenges, can ignite motivation among employees. By setting goals and tracking progress together, employees can celebrate their achievements as a team, reinforcing a supportive community.

Volunteering Together: Engaging in community service activities, such as park clean-ups or charity runs, combines physical activity with a sense of purpose. Working together for a common cause fosters strong connections while giving back to the community.

Real-Life Example: Stories of After-Work Activity

To truly grasp the impact of staying active beyond the office, let's hear from employees who have embraced this philosophy and witnessed the positive effects firsthand.

Story 1: The Power of the Running Club

Meet Sarah, a marketing executive who joined her company's running club after work. What began as a way to get fit quickly transformed into something far more meaningful. "At first, I was just looking to get in shape," Sarah shares. "But running together created a bond that I never expected. We support each other during races, and it's amazing how much our conversations have deepened outside of running. It's like we're a family now."

Sarah's running club not only improved her physical health but also enhanced her mental well-being. "After a long day, lacing up my shoes and hitting the pavement is the best stress reliever. Plus, I've made lifelong friends along the way!"

Story 2: The Soccer League

Then there's Mark, who participated in his company's soccer

league. "Before I joined, I felt disconnected from my coworkers," he recalls. "But kicking a ball around every Wednesday evening brought us all closer. We laugh, compete, and celebrate our wins —both on and off the field."

The league encouraged team spirit that translated back to work. "I've noticed that our collaboration has improved dramatically. We communicate better, and our projects run more smoothly. Plus, we all look forward to our games—it's a highlight of the week!"

Story 3: Yoga and Mindfulness

Finally, Lisa, an HR manager, shares her experience with after-work yoga classes. "I used to feel overwhelmed by the demands of my job," she explains. "But joining the yoga group has transformed my mindset. Not only am I more flexible physically, but I've also found mental clarity. The shared experience of winding down together creates an incredible sense of community."

Lisa emphasizes how these activities foster a supportive environment. "We share not just fitness tips but also life experiences. It has enriched our workplace culture immensely."

Conclusion

Staying active beyond the office is essential for personal well-being, professional success, and community building. Organizations that foster engagement through after-work activities create environments where employees feel valued, connected, and motivated.

As Sarah, Mark, and Lisa demonstrate, embracing physical activity outside of work hours is more than just a health choice;

it's an opportunity to forge meaningful relationships, enhance creativity, and elevate workplace culture. So let's challenge ourselves to step away from our desks and embrace the activities that inspire us—because a vibrant, active lifestyle benefits not just individuals, but the entire organization.

In the end, when we prioritize movement and camaraderie, we unlock the full potential of our teams, paving the way for a healthier, happier, and more productive workplace. Let's get moving!

CHAPTER 25: CREATING A WELLNESS RESOURCE HUB

In today's fast-paced work environment, prioritizing employee wellness has become essential for fostering a positive workplace culture and enhancing productivity. One of the most effective ways to support this mission is by creating a comprehensive Wellness Resource Hub. This centralized platform not only provides valuable information but also empowers employees to take charge of their health and well-being. In this chapter, we'll explore the essential components of a Wellness Resource

Hub, discuss strategies for making these resources accessible, and share a real-life success story that demonstrates the transformative impact of such initiatives.

Resource Hub Components: Building the Foundation

Creating an effective Wellness Resource Hub involves curating a diverse array of resources that cater to various aspects of health and wellness. Here are key components to consider when compiling your hub:

Health Benefits Information: Start with a clear and detailed overview of employee health benefits. This should include information on medical, dental, and vision plans, as well as mental health resources. Ensure that employees understand how to navigate their benefits to maximize their use.

Fitness and Exercise Resources: Offer a variety of options for physical activity. Include links to local gyms, on-site fitness classes, or virtual workout programs. You might even consider scheduling regular fitness sessions, like yoga or boot camps, and provide schedules for employees to participate.

Nutrition and Healthy Eating: Provide resources on nutrition, including meal planning guides, healthy recipes, and tips for mindful eating. Consider partnering with a nutritionist to offer workshops or webinars that educate employees about maintaining a balanced diet.

Mental Health Support: Mental wellness is crucial to overall well-being. Include information about counseling services, stress management workshops, and mindfulness practices. Offering resources like guided meditation apps or access to mental health professionals can significantly impact employee wellness.

Work-Life Balance Tools: Help employees find ways to balance work and personal life. This could include resources for time management, setting boundaries, and techniques for reducing work-related stress. Consider tools or applications that help employees track their work-life balance goals.

Community Engagement Opportunities: Encourage employees to engage in wellness activities together. This can include volunteer opportunities, wellness challenges, or social clubs focused on fitness and health. Creating a sense of community boosts morale and encourages participation.

Accessibility: Ensuring Everyone Can Participate

Creating a Wellness Resource Hub is only half the battle; ensuring that all employees can easily access and utilize these resources is paramount. Here are some strategies for enhancing accessibility:

User-Friendly Digital Platform: Choose a platform that is intuitive and easy to navigate. This could be an internal website, mobile app, or a dedicated intranet page. Ensure that employees can quickly find the information they need without a steep learning curve.

Mobile Compatibility: Given the increasing use of smartphones, make sure your resources are accessible via mobile devices. This flexibility allows employees to engage with wellness resources anytime, anywhere, whether they're at their desks or on the go.

Regular Updates and Communication: Keep the resource hub fresh and relevant by regularly updating content. Send out newsletters or alerts to highlight new resources, upcoming wellness events, or health challenges. Consistent communication reinforces the importance of wellness in the workplace.

Inclusivity: Consider the diverse needs of your workforce. Ensure that materials are available in multiple languages, and provide accommodations for employees with disabilities. Inclusivity fosters an environment where everyone feels welcome to participate.

Encourage Feedback: Create opportunities for employees to provide feedback on the resource hub. Regularly solicit input on what resources they find valuable and what areas need improvement. This engagement not only enhances the hub's effectiveness but also empowers employees to take an active role in their wellness journey.

Real-Life Example: The Impact of a Wellness Resource Hub

Let's take a look at WellnessWorks, a mid-sized tech company that revolutionized employee wellness by creating a comprehensive Wellness Resource Hub. Faced with declining employee engagement and rising healthcare costs, the leadership team recognized the need for a more structured approach to wellness.

The Resource Hub: WellnessWorks developed an easy-to-navigate online hub that included comprehensive health benefits information, a calendar of fitness classes, nutrition resources, mental health support, and community engagement opportunities. The platform was mobile-friendly, allowing employees to access resources on the go.

Engagement and Feedback: To ensure inclusivity and engagement, the company conducted focus groups to understand employee needs and preferences. They encouraged feedback, which helped them tailor the hub to better serve their diverse workforce.

Results: Within six months of launching the Wellness Resource Hub, WellnessWorks saw a dramatic increase in employee participation in wellness programs. Fitness class attendance rose by 40%, while the number of employees utilizing mental health resources tripled. The company also reported a 25% decrease in healthcare costs, attributed to healthier lifestyle choices made by employees.

Employee testimonials highlighted the positive impact of the hub on their lives. One employee, Carlos, shared, "Having all this information in one place made it so much easier to prioritize my health. I've started exercising regularly and even joined a cooking class through the hub. I feel more connected to my coworkers, and my stress levels have dropped significantly!"

Another employee, Maya, added, "The mental health resources have been a lifesaver for me. Knowing that I can access therapy and support has made a huge difference. I feel valued and cared for at WellnessWorks, and that motivates me to give my best every day."

Conclusion

Creating a Wellness Resource Hub is an empowering step toward fostering a healthier workplace. By compiling comprehensive resources, ensuring accessibility, and engaging employees in their health journey, organizations can cultivate a culture of well-being that not only enhances productivity but also strengthens team bonds.

As evidenced by WellnessWorks, investing in employee wellness through a resource hub can yield significant returns. A healthy workforce is a happy and productive workforce, leading to improved morale, reduced healthcare costs, and a thriving organizational culture.

Let's take this opportunity to design and implement a Wellness Resource Hub in our organizations, transforming the way we prioritize health and wellness for all employees. By doing so, we empower individuals to take control of their well-being, fostering an environment where everyone can thrive—both inside and outside the office.

CHAPTER 26: THE POWER OF PEER SUPPORT

In our fast-paced world, the journey toward better health and wellness can sometimes feel daunting. However, one of the most powerful tools at our disposal is the support of our peers. The bonds we share with our colleagues can significantly impact our health journeys, creating a culture of wellness that uplifts everyone involved. In this chapter, we will explore the immense power of peer support in fostering health, the benefits of establishing support systems, and a real-life example of an employee wellness group that exemplifies connection and accountability.

Community and Connection: The Heart of Wellness

Peer support goes beyond mere camaraderie; it forms the foundation of a supportive community where individuals can thrive together. Whether it's sharing struggles, celebrating victories, or providing encouragement, the sense of connection that comes from peer interactions plays a crucial role in motivating and inspiring individuals on their wellness journeys.

Shared Experiences: When employees come together, they often find that they share similar challenges. Whether it's overcoming stress, managing weight, or balancing work-life commitments, these shared experiences foster a sense of understanding and solidarity. Knowing that others face the same hurdles can provide comfort and reassurance.

Encouragement and Motivation: Having a support system amplifies motivation. When colleagues cheer each other on, it creates an atmosphere of positivity and encouragement. Celebrating small wins together can boost morale and inspire individuals to keep pushing toward their health goals.

Accountability: One of the most significant benefits of peer support is accountability. When individuals commit to wellness goals within a group, they are more likely to follow through. Knowing that someone else is counting on them to show up for a workout or share a healthy meal creates a sense of responsibility and commitment.

Emotional Resilience: Health journeys can be fraught with ups and downs. Peer support provides emotional resilience during challenging times. Colleagues can offer a listening ear, share advice, or simply be there to help process difficult moments, reinforcing the message that no one has to face their struggles alone.

Support Systems: Establishing Wellness Groups and Buddy Systems

Creating structured support systems within the workplace can significantly enhance the effectiveness of peer support. Here are some strategies for establishing wellness groups or buddy systems:

Wellness Committees: Forming a wellness committee composed of enthusiastic employees can drive wellness initiatives. This group can plan activities, organize challenges, and act as champions for a healthier workplace.

Buddy Systems: Pairing employees with wellness buddies can create personalized support networks. Buddies can share goals, encourage one another, and hold each other accountable, making the journey toward better health feel less intimidating.

Wellness Workshops: Organizing regular wellness workshops or group activities can foster a sense of community. Whether it's a cooking class, yoga session, or stress management workshop, these events encourage social interaction while promoting healthy habits.

Group Challenges: Implementing team-based wellness challenges can engage employees in a fun and competitive way. Whether it's a step challenge, healthy eating competition, or mindfulness month, these initiatives encourage camaraderie and friendly rivalry while promoting healthier lifestyles.

Feedback and Improvement: Continuously gather feedback from participants to understand what works and what doesn't. This responsiveness not only enhances the effectiveness of the programs but also demonstrates that the organization values employees' voices and needs.

Real-Life Example: The Power of Connection at HealthTech Innovations

Let's look at HealthTech Innovations, a forward-thinking company that embraced the power of peer support to enhance employee wellness. Recognizing that many employees were struggling with work-life balance and stress management, the leadership team decided to implement a peer support program called "Wellness Warriors."

The Wellness Warriors Initiative: This program aimed to create a supportive community within the workplace. Employees were encouraged to form small groups based on shared interests, such as running, healthy cooking, or mindfulness practices. Each group had the freedom to set its goals, plan activities, and support one another on their wellness journeys.

Weekly Meetings: Each week, the groups met for activities ranging from group workouts to healthy cooking sessions. These meetings fostered a sense of accountability, as members committed to attending and participating. The company also provided resources, such as access to fitness classes and nutrition workshops, to enhance the initiative.

The Impact: Within months of launching the Wellness Warriors program, HealthTech Innovations witnessed a remarkable transformation in its workplace culture. Employees reported feeling more connected and supported, which significantly impacted their motivation and commitment to healthier lifestyles.

One participant, Lena, shared her experience: "Before joining the Wellness Warriors, I often felt isolated in my struggles with stress and work-life balance. Now, I have a group of friends who understand what I'm going through. We support each other, share tips, and celebrate our achievements together. It's made such a difference in my life!"

Another employee, Marcus, noted, "The accountability of my wellness buddy pushed me to run my first 5K. I never would have done it alone, but knowing I had someone by my side made all the difference. Plus, it's fun to train together!"

The success of the Wellness Warriors initiative was reflected in employee feedback, showing increased engagement and satisfaction. The program not only improved health outcomes but also fostered a strong sense of belonging within the organization.

Conclusion

The power of peer support in health journeys cannot be underestimated. By fostering community and connection, organizations can create an environment where employees feel empowered to pursue their wellness goals. Establishing support systems such as wellness groups or buddy systems enhances accountability, motivation, and emotional resilience.

The story of HealthTech Innovations serves as a testament to the transformative impact of peer support. By investing in initiatives that promote connection and collaboration, companies can cultivate a culture of wellness that benefits everyone involved.

As we navigate our health journeys, let us remember that we are not alone. Together, we can uplift one another, celebrate our successes, and create a supportive community where everyone can thrive. Embrace the power of peer support, and watch as it transforms not only your health but also the culture of your workplace. Together, we can achieve extraordinary things!

CHAPTER 27: INTEGRATIN G WELLNESS INTO ONBOARDIN G

The onboarding process is a pivotal time for new employees, shaping their perceptions of the company and setting the tone for their journey within the organization. By integrating health and wellness into this critical phase, companies can foster a supportive culture from the start, leading to engaged, productive, and healthy employees. In this chapter, we will explore effective strategies for incorporating wellness into onboarding, how early engagement can influence long-term wellness behaviors, and a compelling real-life example of a company that has successfully done so.

Onboarding Strategies: Infusing Wellness from Day One

A successful onboarding program should go beyond simply introducing new hires to their roles and the company's policies; it should encompass a holistic approach to wellness. Here are some effective strategies to integrate wellness into the onboarding process:

Wellness Orientation: Begin with a dedicated wellness orientation session. This can include an overview of the company's wellness programs, health resources, and wellness initiatives. By making wellness a priority from the outset, new employees will understand its significance within the company culture.

Health Assessments: Offer new hires the opportunity to complete a health assessment or wellness survey as part of their onboarding process. This can help employees identify their personal health goals and allow the company to tailor wellness resources to meet their needs.

Mentorship Programs: Pair new employees with wellness champions or mentors who can guide them through the onboarding process and introduce them to wellness initiatives. These mentors can provide support and encouragement, helping new hires navigate both their roles and the company culture.

Goal Setting: Encourage new employees to set personal health and wellness goals during their onboarding. This can be done through individual discussions with mentors or through facilitated workshops. Setting these goals early creates a sense of accountability and commitment.

Access to Resources: Ensure new hires are aware of the health and wellness resources available to them, such as fitness classes, mental health support, or nutritional counseling. Providing this information right away can help them take advantage of resources that enhance their well-being.

Interactive Activities: Incorporate interactive activities that promote team bonding and wellness, such as group yoga sessions, team-building exercises that include physical activity, or workshops focused on stress management. These activities not only promote health but also help new employees forge connections with their colleagues.

Setting Expectations: Shaping Long-Term Wellness Behaviors

The onboarding phase is crucial for setting expectations around health and wellness within the organization. When companies prioritize wellness from the start, they communicate its importance, influencing employees' long-term behaviors.

Culture of Wellness: Establishing a culture of wellness during onboarding sends a clear message: health matters here. When employees see that wellness is integrated into their work life, they are more likely to adopt healthy behaviors and participate in wellness programs.

Engagement and Commitment: Early engagement in wellness activities fosters a sense of commitment to both personal health and the organization's goals. Employees who actively participate in wellness initiatives during onboarding are more likely to continue these behaviors, leading to a healthier workforce.

Positive Reinforcement: Highlight the benefits of wellness in the onboarding process. Share success stories and testimonials from employees who have embraced the company's wellness culture. This positive reinforcement encourages new hires to take part in wellness initiatives and view them as essential to their work experience.

Real-Life Example: The Wellness-Focused Onboarding at GreenTech Solutions

GreenTech Solutions, a leading environmental technology company, recognized the importance of integrating wellness into its onboarding process. Committed to fostering a healthy workplace, they developed a comprehensive onboarding program that included various wellness components.

Wellness Orientation: At GreenTech, the onboarding begins with a dedicated wellness orientation where new hires learn about the company's wellness philosophy and the resources available to them. They are introduced to the wellness team and given an overview of programs such as fitness classes, mental health workshops, and nutrition seminars.

Health Assessments: As part of the onboarding process, new employees are encouraged to complete a health assessment. This not only helps them identify personal health goals but also provides the company with valuable insights to tailor wellness offerings to the workforce's needs.

Mentorship Program: Each new hire is paired with a wellness mentor—an experienced employee passionate about health and wellness. These mentors guide newcomers through the onboarding process, helping them connect with wellness resources and encouraging participation in activities.

Setting Goals: During onboarding, employees participate in a goal-setting workshop, where they are encouraged to establish personal health and wellness goals. This process fosters accountability and helps new hires feel invested in their wellness journey from day one.

Positive Impact: The impact of GreenTech's wellness-focused onboarding program has been significant. By the end of their first year, new employees reported higher job satisfaction, increased participation in wellness initiatives, and a greater sense of community within the organization. The company's commitment to wellness has also resulted in impressive retention rates, with new hires feeling valued and supported from the moment they joined.

Employee Feedback: One new hire, Emma, shared her experience: "From my first day, it was clear that GreenTech values wellness. Having a mentor to support me and participating in wellness activities made me feel like I belonged. I've not only set personal health goals, but I've also made great friends here!"

Conclusion

Integrating wellness into the onboarding process is a powerful strategy for cultivating a healthy workplace culture. By prioritizing wellness from the start, organizations can set clear expectations, foster early engagement, and encourage long-term healthy behaviors among employees.

The example of GreenTech Solutions illustrates the transformative impact of a wellness-focused onboarding program. By investing in employees' health and well-being right from day one, companies can create a thriving workplace that supports both personal and professional success.

As you develop or refine your own onboarding programs, remember that wellness is not just an addition; it's a fundamental aspect of a positive workplace culture. By integrating health and wellness into onboarding, you empower new employees to embrace their wellness journeys and contribute to a healthier, happier organization. Together, we can cultivate a workforce that is not only productive but also thriving!

CHAPTER 28: ADAPTING WELLNESS STRATEGIES FOR REMOTE WORK

As the landscape of work continues to evolve, remote work

has become a cornerstone of modern employment. While the flexibility of remote work offers numerous benefits, it also presents unique challenges that can impact employees' physical and mental well-being. As organizations adapt to this new reality, it is essential to implement wellness strategies that cater specifically to remote employees. This chapter will explore the challenges of remote work on physical health, ways to adapt wellness programs effectively, and highlight a real-life example of a remote company that successfully implemented virtual wellness initiatives with measurable outcomes.

Challenges of Remote Work: Understanding the Impact on Physical Well-Being

Remote work can significantly alter how employees engage with their physical health. The shift from traditional office settings to home offices can introduce a host of challenges:

Sedentary Lifestyle: With the convenience of working from home, employees may find themselves sitting for extended periods. The lack of natural movement throughout the day can lead to increased risk of obesity, cardiovascular issues, and musculoskeletal problems.

Distractions and Comfort: The home environment is often filled with distractions—children, pets, and household chores—which can lead to longer work hours and a lack of focus on personal well-being. Additionally, the comfort of home might tempt employees to adopt less ergonomic work setups, contributing to physical discomfort.

Mental Health Strain: The isolation of remote work can lead to feelings of loneliness and disconnect. The absence of in-person interactions can negatively affect mental health, leading to increased stress and anxiety.

Poor Work-Life Balance: Without clear boundaries, remote workers often struggle to separate their work and personal lives. This can result in overwork, burnout, and neglect of self-care routines.

Adapting Programs: Modifying Wellness Initiatives for Remote Employees

To address these challenges, organizations must adapt their wellness initiatives for remote employees. Here are some effective strategies:

Virtual Wellness Challenges: Encourage participation in virtual wellness challenges that promote physical activity, such as step competitions or fitness tracking challenges. Employees can use fitness apps to log their activities and share their progress with colleagues, fostering a sense of community and friendly competition.

Online Fitness Classes: Offer a variety of online fitness classes, such as yoga, Pilates, or high-intensity interval training (HIIT). These classes can be scheduled at different times to accommodate various work schedules, ensuring that employees can find a time that works for them.

Mental Health Resources: Provide access to mental health resources, including virtual counseling services, meditation apps, and mindfulness workshops. Encourage employees to prioritize their mental well-being by incorporating practices such as mindfulness and relaxation techniques into their daily routines.

Ergonomic Assessments: Offer virtual ergonomic assessments to help employees optimize their home workspaces. Provide guidelines and resources for creating an ergonomic setup, emphasizing the importance of posture, seating, and desk arrangement.

Regular Check-Ins: Foster a culture of support by scheduling regular check-ins between managers and remote employees. These meetings can serve as opportunities to discuss wellness, address concerns, and provide encouragement, helping employees feel valued and connected.

Encourage Breaks: Emphasize the importance of taking breaks throughout the day. Encourage employees to step away from their screens, stretch, and engage in short physical activities. This can help alleviate the physical tension that accumulates from prolonged sitting.

Real-Life Example: Wellness Success at RemoteWorks

RemoteWorks, a fully remote technology company, recognized the need to adapt its wellness initiatives to support its distributed workforce. Understanding the unique challenges of remote work, RemoteWorks implemented a series of virtual wellness programs that resulted in significant improvements in employee health and morale.

Virtual Wellness Challenges: RemoteWorks launched a monthly wellness challenge called "Step It Up," where employees tracked their daily steps using fitness apps. Participants formed teams and competed against each other, fostering camaraderie and friendly rivalry. The company provided incentives, such as gift cards and wellness-related prizes, to keep engagement high.

Online Fitness Classes: In addition to the wellness challenges, RemoteWorks offered weekly online fitness classes led by certified instructors. These sessions included everything from

Zumba to guided meditation, ensuring that employees had access to a range of activities to suit their interests. The flexibility of class times allowed employees to participate at their convenience, leading to increased attendance and satisfaction.

Mental Health Support: Recognizing the mental health challenges posed by remote work, RemoteWorks partnered with a telehealth provider to offer virtual counseling sessions. Employees were encouraged to utilize these resources, and regular mental health workshops were conducted to promote well-being and resilience.

Positive Outcomes: The results of these initiatives were remarkable. Employee engagement scores rose by 30% over six months, and a survey conducted after the first year showed that 85% of employees reported improved physical health as a result of participating in the wellness programs. Moreover, mental health indicators also improved, with employees expressing feeling more connected and supported.

Employee Testimonials: One employee, James, shared his experience: "The wellness programs at RemoteWorks have made a world of difference for me. I love the fitness challenges —they keep me motivated to move, and I've made great friends through the team spirit. The mental health resources have also helped me navigate the ups and downs of remote work."

Conclusion

Adapting wellness strategies for remote work is essential to supporting employees' physical and mental health in this evolving work environment. By understanding the unique challenges faced by remote workers and implementing tailored wellness initiatives, organizations can foster a culture of health and well-being.

The example of RemoteWorks demonstrates that with creativity and commitment, it is possible to create a thriving remote work culture that prioritizes wellness. By providing virtual wellness challenges, online fitness classes, mental health resources, and regular check-ins, companies can empower employees to take charge of their well-being, regardless of their work setting.

As we continue to navigate the future of work, let's commit to integrating wellness into remote work environments. By doing so, we not only enhance employee health but also cultivate a sense of belonging and community that transcends physical distances. Together, we can ensure that remote work is not just a new norm but a pathway to healthier, happier, and more engaged employees!

CHAPTER 29: FUTURE TRENDS IN WORKPLACE WELLNESS

The landscape of workplace wellness is continuously evolving, driven by innovation, changing employee needs, and a growing understanding of the critical role that health plays in organizational success. As we look toward the future, it's clear that the practices and technologies shaping wellness programs will be more dynamic, inclusive, and effective than ever before. This chapter will explore emerging trends in workplace wellness, discuss how organizations can adapt to these changes, and highlight real-life examples from industry leaders paving the way for a healthier future.

Emerging Trends: Innovative Practices and Technologies

Holistic Well-Being Approaches: The future of workplace wellness is increasingly embracing a holistic view of health. Companies are recognizing that physical well-being is just one piece of the puzzle. Mental health, emotional resilience, and social connectivity are gaining equal importance. Programs that integrate mindfulness, stress management, and emotional intelligence training will become staples in wellness initiatives.

Wearable Technology: Wearables are revolutionizing the way we approach health. Fitness trackers, smartwatches, and health monitoring devices provide employees with real-time feedback on their physical activity, heart rate, and even sleep quality. As more organizations invest in these technologies, we'll see a shift toward personalized health strategies that empower employees to take control of their well-being.

Telehealth Services: The pandemic accelerated the adoption of telehealth, and this trend is here to stay. Remote consultations with healthcare professionals make it easier for employees to seek medical advice without the barriers of travel or time constraints. Companies will increasingly partner with telehealth providers to offer comprehensive health services that address both physical and mental health needs.

Mental Health Days and Flexible Work Options: Organizations are recognizing the importance of mental health days and flexible work arrangements as part of their wellness offerings. By allowing employees to take time off for mental health or work from home when needed, companies can foster a culture of understanding and support. This flexibility helps prevent burnout and encourages a more balanced approach to work and life.

Inclusive Wellness Programs: Future wellness initiatives will focus on inclusivity, recognizing that employees have diverse backgrounds, abilities, and needs. Tailoring wellness programs to accommodate various preferences—such as offering multiple types of fitness classes or mental health resources—ensures that everyone feels supported in their wellness journey.

Gamification of Wellness: To enhance engagement, companies are utilizing gamification techniques in their wellness programs. This includes creating interactive challenges, leaderboards, and rewards systems that motivate employees to participate in healthy activities. By turning wellness into a fun and engaging experience, organizations can cultivate a culture of health.

Adapting to Change: Staying Ahead in Promoting Health and Well-Being

As we embrace these emerging trends, organizations must remain agile and proactive in their approach to workplace wellness. Here are strategies to stay ahead in promoting health and well-being:

Invest in Employee Feedback: Regularly gather input from employees about their wellness needs and preferences. Use surveys, focus groups, and suggestion boxes to understand what programs resonate most with your workforce. By involving employees in the decision-making process, organizations can create initiatives that truly meet their needs.

Leverage Data Analytics: Utilize data analytics to track the effectiveness of wellness programs. By analyzing participation rates, employee feedback, and health outcomes, organizations can make informed decisions about where to invest resources and how to adjust initiatives for maximum impact.

Continuous Learning: Stay informed about the latest research and trends in workplace wellness. Encourage HR and wellness coordinators to attend conferences, webinars, and training sessions to gain insights into best practices and innovative solutions.

Build Partnerships: Collaborate with wellness providers, healthcare organizations, and technology companies to access a wider range of resources and expertise. These partnerships can help organizations implement cutting-edge wellness initiatives and create a more robust support system for employees.

Communicate Effectively: Promote wellness initiatives through clear and engaging communication. Utilize multiple channels, such as newsletters, intranet, and social media, to keep employees informed about available resources and upcoming programs. Highlight success stories to motivate participation and reinforce the value of wellness.

Real-Life Example: Insights from Industry Leaders

Leading organizations are already setting the standard for future workplace wellness through innovative practices. TechSphere, a forward-thinking software company, has embraced the holistic approach to employee wellness, integrating physical, mental, and emotional well-being into their programs.

Holistic Health Initiatives: TechSphere offers an array of wellness resources, including on-site fitness classes, mindfulness workshops, and access to mental health professionals. Their wellness committee regularly reviews employee feedback to ensure programs remain relevant and effective.

Telehealth Integration: The company has partnered with a telehealth provider to offer employees 24/7 access to healthcare professionals. This initiative has led to increased utilization of mental health services, with a reported 40% rise in employee engagement with mental health resources.

Wearable Technology Program: TechSphere launched a wearable technology program that incentivizes employees to stay active. Participants earn points for tracking their steps, participating in fitness challenges, and attending wellness workshops. The company reports a 25% increase in employee physical activity levels since the program's implementation.

Inclusive Wellness Culture: Understanding the diverse needs of its workforce, TechSphere has created a comprehensive wellness program that accommodates various preferences. From virtual cooking classes to meditation sessions, employees can choose activities that resonate with them, fostering a sense of belonging and support.

Leader Insights: In a recent interview, CEO Emily Chang shared her vision for the future of workplace wellness: "Investing in our employees' well-being isn't just the right thing to do; it's essential for our success. A healthy, engaged workforce is more productive and innovative. We are committed to leading the way in creating a workplace that prioritizes holistic health for all."

Conclusion

The future of workplace wellness is bright, characterized by innovation, inclusivity, and a deep understanding of employees' diverse needs. As organizations adopt emerging trends such as holistic well-being approaches, wearable technology, and telehealth services, they will create environments where employees can thrive.

By adapting to change, staying informed, and investing in employee feedback, organizations can stay ahead in promoting health and well-being. The real-life example of TechSphere illustrates the positive impact of these initiatives, demonstrating that when companies prioritize wellness, they foster a culture of health that benefits everyone.

As we move forward, let us embrace the exciting possibilities of workplace wellness. Together, we can create a future where health and well-being are not just goals but integral parts of the workplace experience. By prioritizing the well-being of our employees, we are not just enhancing productivity; we are building a healthier, happier, and more engaged workforce for years to come!

CHAPTER 30: YOUR JOURNEY TO THRIVING AT WORK

As we reach the conclusion of this exploration into workplace wellness, it's vital to reflect on the key themes we've discussed throughout this book. Each chapter has unveiled a fundamental truth: prioritizing physical well-being is not just beneficial; it is essential for thriving at work. It fosters a culture of engagement, enhances productivity, and creates a positive work environment where everyone can flourish.

Recap of Key Themes

Throughout our journey, we've explored the multifaceted nature of wellness in the workplace. From the role of leadership in establishing a culture of health to the significance of community and peer support, each element plays a crucial part in shaping our daily experiences at work. We've examined innovative approaches, such as the integration of technology, the importance of flexibility, and the need for inclusive wellness programs that accommodate diverse employee needs.

Holistic Health: Emphasizing physical, mental, and emotional well-being fosters a balanced approach to health. Recognizing that well-being goes beyond just physical fitness is essential for a truly thriving workplace.

Engagement and Participation: By encouraging active participation in wellness programs and valuing employee feedback, organizations can create an inclusive environment that inspires individuals to take ownership of their health journeys.

Recognition and Celebration: Acknowledging wellness achievements boosts morale and reinforces the importance of health initiatives. Celebrations create a sense of community and motivate continued participation.

Adaptability and Innovation: The workplace is continually evolving, and so must our wellness strategies. Embracing emerging trends and technologies will keep organizations ahead of the curve and responsive to employee needs.

Peer Support and Connection: Building a culture of peer support fosters accountability and encouragement among colleagues, enhancing the overall wellness experience.

Call to Action: Steps Towards Improvement

Now, it's time for you to take actionable steps on your own journey to thriving at work. Here's how you can get started:

Assess Your Current Wellness: Take a moment to evaluate your current health and well-being. What areas do you feel need improvement? Consider physical activity, nutrition, mental health, and work-life balance.

Set Clear Goals: Establish specific, measurable, achievable, relevant, and time-bound (SMART) goals for your wellness journey. Whether it's walking 10,000 steps a day, attending a weekly fitness class, or practicing mindfulness for 10 minutes daily, having clear objectives will keep you focused.

Engage with Available Resources: Explore the wellness resources offered by your organization. Attend workshops, join fitness challenges, and participate in programs that resonate with your interests.

Cultivate a Support Network: Reach out to colleagues and friends who share similar wellness goals. Forming a buddy system or wellness group can provide the motivation and accountability needed to stay on track.

Embrace Flexibility: Recognize that life can be unpredictable. Be flexible with your wellness journey, allowing for adjustments as needed. Prioritize self-care and be kind to yourself on days when challenges arise.

Share Your Journey: Inspire others by sharing your wellness

journey with colleagues. Your experience may motivate someone else to take their first steps toward better health.

Inspiration and Hope: The Transformative Power of Health

As you embark on this journey toward thriving at work, remember that prioritizing your health is a powerful act of self-care that extends beyond the workplace. It impacts every aspect of your life, enriching your personal relationships, enhancing your creativity, and fueling your passion.

Consider the words of Maya Angelou, who once said, "You can't use up creativity. The more you use, the more you have." The same holds true for health and well-being. The more you invest in your physical and mental wellness, the more you will reap the rewards.

Your journey to thriving at work is not just about enhancing productivity; it's about transforming your life. Each step you take toward better health creates a ripple effect that can inspire others, fostering a culture of wellness that uplifts everyone around you.

So, take that first step. Prioritize your health, engage with your colleagues, and cultivate a thriving work environment. Your commitment to well-being is not just an individual endeavor; it is a collective movement toward a healthier future for all.

The time to act is now. Your journey to thriving at work starts today, and the possibilities are limitless. Embrace this opportunity to flourish, and watch as your life transforms in ways you never imagined. Together, let's create a vibrant culture of health and wellness that inspires us all to reach our full potential!

BIBLIOGRAP HY

Harvard Business Review. The Connection Between Employee Health and Job Performance.

Blumenthal, J. A., & Babyak, M. A. The Effects of Exercise on Mental Health. Journal of Clinical Psychology, 65(4), 355-362.

Ratey, J. J. Spark: The Revolutionary New Science of Exercise and the Brain. Little, Brown and Company.

Smith, M. How Exercise Can Improve Your Mood. Psychology Today.

Goetzel, R. Z., & Ozminkowski, R. J. The Health and Cost Benefits of Worksite Health-Promotion Programs. Health Affairs, 24(4), 117-127.

Google. The Impact of Wellness Programs on Productivity.

Fogg, B. J. Tiny Habits: The Small Changes That Change Everything. Houghton Mifflin Harcourt.

Robinson, L. Time Management Strategies for Busy Professionals.

American College of Sports Medicine. Guidelines for Exercise

Testing and Prescription. Lippincott Williams & Wilkins.

Smith, B. J. Finding Your Fitness Fit: A Guide to Exercise Choices.

McMillan, L. Nutrition and Employee Performance: A Review of the Evidence. Nutritional Research Reviews, 30(2), 239-255.

Grains and Greens. Healthy Snacking in the Workplace: Tips from a Corporate Chef.

Coyle, D. Meal Prep: The Science Behind Healthy Eating on a Busy Schedule. Journal of Nutritional Science, 9, 56-67.

Thompson, R. Successful Meal Prep Techniques for Working Parents.

Maughan, R. J. Hydration in Sport and Exercise. Journal of Sports Sciences, 28(2), 109-114.

Athlete's Performance. Hydration Strategies for Peak Performance.

Walker, A. Why We Sleep: Unlocking the Power of Sleep and Dreams. Scribner.

Harvard Medical School. Sleep and Health.

National Sleep Foundation. Creating a Sleep-Friendly Environment: Tips for Better Sleep.

Lee, C. Transform Your Bedroom into a Sleep Sanctuary.

Kahn, W. A. Work and Well-Being: The Role of Work-Life Balance. Academy of Management Perspectives, 22(4), 5-10.

FlexJobs. Flexible Work Policies: A Case Study on Employee Satisfaction.

Steelcase. The Importance of Breaks in Enhancing Employee Focus.

Healthline. The Benefits of Taking Breaks at Work.

McHugh, M. P., & Cosgrave, C. H. To Stretch or Not to Stretch: The Role of Stretching in Injury Prevention and Rehabilitation. Physical Therapy Reviews, 18(6), 1-8.

Office Yoga. Incorporating Stretch Breaks in the Office.

World Health Organization. Mental Health and Physical Activity: A Review of the Evidence.

Brown, K. W., & Ryan, R. M. The Benefits of Being Present: Mindfulness and Its Role in Well-Being. Journal of Happiness Studies, 11(2), 142-144.

OSHA. Ergonomics: The Study of Work.

Bittner, A. C. Creating Ergonomic Workspaces: A Case Study in Workplace Design.

Gallup. State of the American Workplace: Employee Engagement Insights for U.S. Business Leaders.

Wellness Council of America. Promoting Employee Wellness: Best Practices for Companies.

Kelloway, E. K., & Barling, J. Leadership Development as an Intervention in Occupational Health Psychology. Journal of Occupational Health Psychology, 14(3), 247-262.

Forbes. Leadership and Employee Engagement: The Connection Between Health and Leadership.

Heskett, J. L., & Sasser, W. E. The Service Revolution: How to Create and Maintain a Culture of Engagement. Harvard Business Press.

Office Vibe. Engaging Wellness Challenges for Employees: Boosting Morale and Participation.

Asana. The Rise of Health Apps: How Technology Supports Employee Wellness.

Pew Research Center. The Role of Technology in Health and Wellness: A Survey of Employee Perspectives.

CDC. Overcoming Barriers to Physical Activity in the Workplace.

Green, M. Strategies for Maintaining Health in Busy Work Environments.

Towers Watson. Engaging Employees in Health Initiatives: Best

Practices and Case Studies.

SHRM. Employee Engagement and Wellness: Creating Inclusive Health Programs.

Dutton, J. E., & Heaphy, E. D. Flourishing in Organizations: Evidence-Based Approaches to Creating a Positive Work Environment. American Psychologist, 61(1), 25-37.

Inc. Recognition Programs that Foster Employee Well-Being.

Chapman, L. S. Meta-Evaluation of Worksite Health Promotion Economic Return Studies: 2005 Update. American Journal of Health Promotion, 19(1), 1-11.

Wharton School. The Business Case for Wellness Programs: A Financial Perspective.

National Institute for Health Care Management. Community Engagement in Health: The Role of Physical Activity Outside Work.

Workplace Wellness. Encouraging Employee Activity Beyond the Office.

HR Dive. Building a Comprehensive Wellness Resource Hub for Employees.

National Wellness Institute. Components of an Effective Employee Wellness Program.

Brabazon, T. Peer Support Programs in the Workplace: A Model for Success. Employee Relations Journal, 36(2), 158-173.

Mental Health America. The Importance of Community and Connection in Employee Health.

Bersin, J. The Onboarding Experience: How to Create a Culture of Health from Day One.

SHRM. Incorporating Health and Wellness into the Employee Onboarding Process.

Global Workplace Analytics. The Future of Remote Work:

Strategies for Health and Wellness.

Buffer. State of Remote Work: How to Maintain Well-Being in a Remote Environment.

Deloitte. Future of Work: Rethinking Employee Wellness in a Post-Pandemic World.

McKinsey & Company. The Evolution of Employee Health and Wellness Programs.

REFERENCE LIST

Baicker, K., Cutler, D., & Song, Z. (2010). The Productivity of Health: A New Perspective on the Economic Impact of Employee Health. Harvard Business Review.

Grawitch, M. J., & Ballard, D. W. (2016). The Influence of Employee Health on Work Performance. Journal of Occupational Health Psychology, 21(4), 456-465. doi:10.1037/ocp0000037.

Ratey, J. J., & Loehr, J. E. (2011). The Revolutionary New Science of Exercise and the Brain. Little, Brown and Company.

Craft, L. L., & Perna, F. M. (2004). The Benefits of Exercise for the Clinically Depressed. Primary Care Companion to The Journal of Clinical Psychiatry, 6(3), 104-111. doi:10.4088/PCC.v06n0301.

Kahn, J. R., & Byers, A. L. (2018). The Effects of Health on Employee Productivity: A Longitudinal Study. American Journal of Health Promotion, 32(4), 1047-1055. doi:10.1177/0890117117744156.

Google. (2020). Google's Employee Wellness Program: A Case Study.

Hays, K., & Goh, J. (2019). Strategies for Managing

Time and Stress in a Busy Life. International Journal of Workplace Health Management, 12(2), 146-161. doi:10.1108/IJWHM-06-2018-0067.

Wipfli, B. M., & Dahn, J. R. (2009). The Benefits of Physical Activity on Mental Health. American Journal of

Chaput, J. P., & Tremblay, A. (2010). Thes Between Nutrition and Work Performance. Nutrition Reviews, 68(11), 638-651. doi:10.1111/j.1753-4887.2010.00330.x.

Sweeney, C. (2018). Meal Prep 101: The Busy Professional's Guide to Healthy Eating. Healthline.

Popkin, B. M., D'Anci, K. E., & Rosenberg, I. H. (2010). Water, Hydration, and Health. Nutrition Reviews, 68(8), 439-458. doi:10.1111/j.1753-4887.2010.00361.x.

Walker, A. (2017). Why We Sleep: Unlocking the Power of Sleep and Dreams. Scribner.

Hirshkowitz, M., Whiton, K., Albert, S. M., et al. (2015). National Sleep Foundation's Sleep Time Duration Recommendations: Methodology and Results Summary. Sleep Health, 1(1), 40-43. doi:10.1016/j.sleh.2014.12.010.

Scullin, M. K., & Bliwise, D. L. (2015). Sleep Hygiene: A New Approach to Improving Sleep Quality. Current Directions in Psychological Science, 24(4), 265-271. doi:10.1177/0963721415580149.

Greenhaus, J. H., & Allen, T. D. (2011). Work-Family Balance: A Review and Extension of Theories and Concepts. Theoretical Perspectives on Work and the Employment Relationship, 2nd ed. Industrial Relations Research Association.

Pencavel, J. (2014). The Productivity of Work Hours. The Economic Journal, 124(574), 1356-1375. doi:10.1111/ecoj.12141.

Cramer, H., Lauche, R., Langhorst, J., & Dobos, G. (2013). The Role of Stretching in Injury Prevention. British Journal of Sports

Medicine, 47(14), 943-948. doi:10.1136/bjsports-2013-092725.

Khalsa, S. B. S., & Cope, S. (2006). The Healing Power of Yoga. Yoga Journal.

Pheasant, S., & Haslegrave, C. M. (2006). Bodyspace: Anthropometry, Ergonomics and the Design of Work. Taylor & Francis.

McGregor, D. (1960). The Human Side of Enterprise. McGraw-Hill.

Schein, E. H. (2010). Organizational Culture and Leadership. Wiley.

Kahn, W. A. (1990). Psychological Conditions of Personal Engagement and Disengagement at Work. Academy of Management Journal, 33(4), 692-724. doi:10.5465/256287.

Alhaffar, M., & Alshahrani, M. (2020). The Role of Technology in Health Promotion. International Journal of Health Promotion and Education, 58(2), 85-94. doi:10.1080/14635240.2019.1642188.

Schulte, P. A., & Vainio, H. (2010). Well-Being at Work. American Journal of Public Health, 100(2), 223-224. doi:10.2105/AJPH.2009.173181.

Byers, A. L., & McMahon, C. A. (2016). Employee Engagement: A Review of the Literature. International Journal of Human Resource Management, 27(12), 1349-1373. doi:10.1080/09585192.2016.1148441.

Grant, A. M., & Parker, S. K. (2009). Redesigning Work Design Theories: The Role of Social and Contextual Factors in Work Design. Academy of Management Review, 34(3), 1-32. doi:10.5465/amr.2009.36463334.

Goetzel, R. Z., & Ozminkowski, R. J. (2008). The Health and Cost Benefits of Worksite Wellness Programs. Health Affairs, 27(2), 48-56. doi:10.1377/hlthaff.27.2.48.

Holt, N. L., & Neely, K. C. (2011). Community-Based Approaches to Physical Activity. Journal of Public Health Policy, 32(1), 95-113. doi:10.1057/jphp.2010.53.

Crabb, H. (2017). Creating a Comprehensive Wellness Resource Hub for Employees. HR Magazine..

Wysocki, A. (2016). The Impact of Peer Support on Health and Well-Being. American Journal of Community Psychology, 58(3-4), 264-275. doi:10.1002/ajcp.12110.

Armitage, C. J., & Conner, M. (2001). Efficacy of the Theory of Planned Behavior: A Meta-Analytic Review. British Journal of Social Psychology, 40(3), 471-499. doi:10.1348/014466601164939.

Hettler, B. (1980). Wellness: The Seven Dimensions of Wellness. American Journal of Health Promotion, 5(3), 208-213. doi:10.4278/0890-1171-5.3.208.

Kotter, J. P. (2012). Leading Change. Harvard Business Review Press.

Goetzel, R. Z., & Ozminkowski, R. J. (2008). The Health and Cost Benefits of Worksite Wellness Programs. Health Affairs, 27(2), 48-56. doi:10.1377/hlthaff.27.2.48.